Fryderyck Franciszek Chopin

Illustrated **Lives of the Great Composers**

Ateş Orga

OMNIBUS PRESS

London | New York | Sydney | Copenhagen | Berlin | Madrid | Tokyo

© 2015 Ateş D'Arcy-Orga.

Cover designed by Zach John Design.
Picture research by Sarah Datblygu.

ISBN: 978-1-78038-444-3
. Order No: OP54626

Exclusive Distributors
Music Sales Limited,
14/15 Berners Street,
London, W1T 3LJ, United Kingdom.

Music Sales Corporation,
257 Park Avenue South,
New York, NY 10010, USA.

Macmillan Distribution Services,
56 Parkwest Drive
Derrimut, Vic 3030, Australia.

Every effort has been made to trace the copyright holders of photographs and quotations in this book but one or two were unreachable. We should be grateful if any photographers or copyright holders concerned would please contact us.

Printed in the EU.

A catalogue record for this book is available from the British Library.

Visit Omnibus Press on the web at www.omnibuspress.com

Illustrated **Lives of the Great Composers**

Bach (Tim Dowley)
Chopin (Ateş Orga)
Debussy (Paul Holmes)
Liszt (Bryce Morrison)
Mahler (Edward Seckerson)

Contents

For Isabelle

Author's Note

I first drafted this book as a student in the mid-sixties, guided by my late parents and especially my father, İrfan Orga. It was published in Tunbridge Wells in 1976. My original acknowledgements credited the support and encouragement of Arthur Hedley (1905-69) and Maurice J E Brown (1906-75), who in their time brought fresh standards of scholarship to Chopin research in post-war Britain. Thanks went also to Josephine Orga (Leak), Adam Harasowski, Baron Sachlan Linden, and my publishers at Midas Books, Kathleen and Ian Morley-Clarke. Post-publication, my students at the University of Surrey – more especially Susan W. Roberts and Sarah Plummer – were to have valued critical input. Some of their ideas and suggestions are implemented in the present revision. Hours of provocative discussion with Nelly Akopian-Tamarina have yielded immeasurable insights since.

A.O.
Arcueil, Paris
May 2014

Also by Ateş Orga

The Proms (1974)
Beethoven: His Life and Times (1978)

Essayist

Falla and Spanish Tradition Gervase Hughes & Herbert van Thal (eds.) *The Music Lover's Companion* (1971)
Charles Camilleri Richard England (ed.) *Contemporary Art in Malta* (1973)
Roberto Gerhard: The Works, the Man and His Music David Atherton (ed.) *Schoenberg/Gerhard Series: The Complete Instrumental and Chamber Music* (1973)
Alan Bush: The Concertos Ronald Stevenson (ed.) *Time Remembered* (1981)
İrfan Orga: Portrait of a Turkish Family – Afterword (1988 rev 2011)
İrfan Orga: The Caravan Moves On – Afterword (2002)
İrfan Orga: Dark Journey – Afterword (2014)
Sebastian Forbes: A Conversation Peter O'Hagan (ed.) *Aspects of British Music of the 1990s* (2003)
Flight, Flame, Farewell Barnaby Rogerson (ed.) *Meetings with Remarkable Muslims* (2005)
Ronald Stevenson: The Piano Music Colin Scott-Sutherland (ed.) *Ronald Stevenson: The Man and His Music* (2005)
Dreaming of the Bosphorus Gail Pirkis & Hazel Wood (eds.) *Slightly Foxed* No. 37 (2013)
İrfan Orga: Dark Journey - Afterword (2014)

Anthologist

Istanbul: Poetry of Place (2007 rev. 2012)

Editor

Records & Recording Classical Guide 77 (1977)
Records & Recording Classical Guide 78 – with Josephine Orga (1978)

http://www.atesorga.co.uk

I. Childhood

'Not so much a musician as a soul'

Honoré de Balzac

Chopin: oil portrait by Delacroix, July-August 1838, unfinished. Sketched and painted at the artist's Paris *atelier*, 17 rue des Marais, Saint-Germain, with a Pleyel piano brought in for the sittings. 'If the mighty autocrat of the north knew what a dangerous enemy threatened him in Chopin's compositions, in the simple tunes of his mazurkas, he would forbid this music. Chopin's works are cannons buried in flowers' - Robert Schumann.

Legends are made, heroes are born… They are the stuff of history, of imagination. They are man's inheritance, his legacy, the inspiration of generations. Fryderyk Franciszek Chopin was such a legend, such a hero. One of Poland's supreme sons he was to become synonymous with the country itself. His mazurkas and polonaises became the spirit incarnate of the Polish people and plain. Years after his death his music retained its alchemic genius. For millions it came to be a symbol of freedom and liberation – never more so perhaps than for those Poles during the Second World War who remembered that Chopin himself had penned much of it as an exile in Paris while Russia's occupying might shackled the motherland. When Szymanowski's brother-in-law, Jarosław Iwaszkiewicz, published his life of Chopin in 1955, he summed up better than most what Chopin has come to mean today:

> His work has remained, to endure and increase in its scope and influence with the passage of time, entering ever more intimately into the lives of men, revealing new riches every day, and growing every day more and more indispensable. It expresses the struggles and the sufferings of every one of us and forms a rainbow bridge between Poland and the rest of the world. It remains as the finest art Poland has ever produced.

Chopin was born in the village of Żelazowa Wola, to the west of Warsaw, on 1 March 1810 *. His birthplace – the left-wing of an original manor house burnt down in 1814 – still stands, today a museum dedicated to his memory. Long and low, with flowers and rambling plants surrounding the windows and porch, it reposes in a large garden, a group of tall trees offering shade and relieving the monotony of plains stretching to the horizon. A stream flows nearby, in the heat of summer murmuring softly, a haven of cool rest, in winter frozen and silent. In Chopin's day the house

* This was the date recognised by the family; the birth certificate (23 April) gives 22 February, 'at six o'clock in the evening'. Chopin's name-day was celebrated on 5 March.

belonged to Countess Ludwika Skarbek, divorced in 1806, for whom Chopin's parents, Nicholas and Justyna, worked in a spirit of familiarity *.

Nicholas [Mikołaj] (1771-1844) was born in Marainville, nestling among the sunny vine-growing provinces of Lorraine in eastern France. The son of peasant stock, his father (a wheelwright by trade) and grandfather owned extensive vineyards, and the family appears to have been long established in the area. When Nicholas was a boy his village belonged to a Polish nobleman, Michał Jan Pac, who may have come to the area when Stanisław I, King of Poland, was made Duke of Lorraine in 1735. Nicholas was accordingly familiar with Poles from an early age, and was popular with several members of Pac's staff, including Adam Weydlicj, responsible for organising and running the count's estates.

Cleverer than the rest of his family – whose women could neither read nor write – he took the opportunity in 1787, aged sixteen, to travel to Poland with Weydlicj, whom he had begun to help in the administration of Pac's affairs and business. Young as he was, he was highly regarded and trusted by his superiors. He became adept at dealing with financial problems, and his command of Polish and French, later German, stood him in good stead as well as being a starry achievement for someone of such modest origins.

Nicholas liked the atmosphere he found in Warsaw and used his talent for figures to become an apprentice clerk in a tobacco factory. So long, too, as he remained in Poland, he avoided conscription into the French army – crucial at a time when France was seething with unrest, on the verge of the most epic revolution in modern history. In his only surviving letter, to his parents (15 September 1790), Nicholas observes that 'being in a foreign country where I can pursue my own small career I should be sorry to leave it to become a soldier, even if it were for my country'. Ultimately though he wasn't to be spared the stresses and suffering of the French Revolution, for the symbol it embodied – democratic freedom – became the call-to-arms of a European generation. The Polish-Lithuanian Commonwealth, partitioned twice since 1772 between Russia, Prussia and, subsequently, Austria, needed little encouragement to follow suit – with the result that one day in late March 1794 Nicholas found his routine dramatically interrupted when the Polish National Cavalry staged an uprising protesting the 1793 second partition, targeting Russian (later also Prussian) forces. By now Nicholas

* 'The relations between Ludwika and the Chopins can be defined as those between employer and employee, yet with a distinct degree of domestic intimacy, with a certain blurring of the differences in social and material status' (Piotr Mysłakowski, Andrzej Sikorski, 2006).

Chopin's birthplace. Presumed originally to have been shingle-thatched.

was more and more committed to Polish independence, and was losing interest in France. He joined the compulsory Residents' Militia, distinguished himself, and rose to the rank of captain. But by November Tadeusz Kościuszko and his insurrectionists were crushed and Warsaw was allocated to the Prussians. Nicholas was despondent. He had no money, the tobacco factory no longer existed, and he thought of returning to France. Illness, however, prevented him: 'Twice I have tried to leave,' he said, 'and twice I have nearly died. I must bow before the will of providence and I will stay.' His decision was final: he severed what tenuous links there were with his homeland and in later years kept all knowledge from his children of his French birthright and humble beginnings. He even declared France to be a 'foreign' country.

For the first few years Nicholas's knowledge of French and Polish proved useful and he taught the children of various aristocratic families, finally in 1802 accepting a post as tutor with Countess Ludwika – effectively a single mother in her late thirties. Here, 'a moral, honest man' with a partiality for Voltaire, he met his future wife, Justyna Krzyżanowska (1782-1861), a quiet, educated girl in her early twenties, a 'very distant' relation of the Skarbek family. Blond and blue-eyed, she was said to have sung and played the piano well. She evidently pleased Nicholas, who had an ear for music and himself played flute and violin. Matched

Chopin's sister Ludwika (1807-55) and his parents Justyna (1782-1861) and Nicholas (1771-1844): oil portraits by Ambroży Mieroszewski, 1829.

* The Chopin family lived in tied accommodation – firstly in the Saski (Saxon) Palace (1810-17, blown up in 1944), then Kazimierz Palace (1817-27, destroyed 1939/44). In the summer of 1827 they moved to Krasiński (Czapski) Palace (burnt down 1944), at which point they ceased taking in boarders. 'Upstairs there is a [garret] room that is to serve my comfort... There I am to have an old piano and an old bureau; it is to be my own place of refuge' (27 December 1828). Kazimierz and Krasiński were reconstructed and restored post-1945.

by the Countess, they were 'splendidly' married in the village of Brochów in June 1806 and had four children: Ludwika Marianna [Louise], Fryderyk Franciszek [Frédéric François], Justyna Izabela [Isabella] and Emilia. Izabela, always intensely proud of her brother's gift, lived the longest – she died in 1881 – while Emilia was taken by consumption at the age of fourteen. Ludwika, emotionally and temperamentally close to Fryderyk, died six years after him.

With his father's looks and features, Chopin was a sensitive, poetic child, qualities inherited from his mother, and he was brought up in Warsaw where his parents had moved shortly after his birth. Remembered as 'a man of rigid moral standards, meticulous, just, hard-working and demanding [enjoying] a considerable prestige in Warsaw élite circles' (Piotr Sikorski), his father was a collaborator then titular Professor of French at the Lyceum (Gymnasium, High School) from 1810 to 1832. He also took up various extra-curricular teaching appointments, helping to offset the cost of living a life of pleasant material wealth in the most fashionable part of the city *. During these years Warsaw was part of the Duchy of Warsaw formed by Napoléon in 1807. To the young Chopin the Napoléonic age meant little or nothing, though it coloured and shaped an era. Terror and tragedy smouldered on distant horizons, Napoléon's armies marched bravely on doomed campaigns, but Warsaw remained a comparatively isolated satellite state. By 1814–15, when the Congress of Vienna met to re-organise a broken Europe, Poland was divided up yet again, with Warsaw becoming the capital of the region controlled by the Russians who had re-occupied the city in January 1813.

Above: Izabela Chopin (1811-81): oil portrait by Ambroży Mieroszewski, 1829.

Below: Old Warsaw, with the Conservatoire on the left: aquatint by Fryderyk Dietrich. In 1816 the population was estimated at around 81,000, nearly a fifth of whom were Jewish. By 1821 it had increased to 140,000. More than 85% of the city was destroyed by Reich forces during the Second World War.

His father's keen judgement and logic were important in moulding Chopin, whose upbringing and family values ensured, too, that he was well mannered, with all the social graces. He was an aristocrat by instinct, something which never ceased to surprise his contemporaries. In those days musicians were still frequently viewed as little more than servants, a legacy of earlier times when composers like Sebastian Bach, Domenico Scarlatti or Haydn were in the employ of rich patrons or the church. Never mind that Beethoven had shaken a mighty fist and broken the bondage chain. Being a 'piano player' – society largely agreed – a trapeze artist purveying entertainment in exchange for money, simply wasn't what a gentleman of class did…

Chopin's love of music showed itself early. According to Izabela, when his mother and Ludwika played dances on the grand piano, or accompanied his father, he would 'display a sensitivity to musical impressions by crying'. With Ludwika's help he began to explore the keyboard for himself and delighted in experimenting. By the age of six he'd become sufficiently good for his parents to find him a teacher. Their choice fell on Adalbert [Wojciech] Żywny, a yellow-wigged, snuff-taking, frock-coated, pencil wielding Bohemian-born composer then aged sixty-one.

He was a competent musician, who for six years instilled a reverence for the works of Bach and Mozart. He encouraged his charge to explore the great Viennese masters, as well as more

Adalbert Żywny (1756-1842): oil portrait by Ambroży Mieroszewski.

fashionable pieces by lesser men, and ensured a solid grounding in the rudiments of music. Żywny's approach was ideally affectionate and understanding.

Chopin even so had a will of his own: practising the piano, he amused himself more with improvisation and making up pieces than playing scales or finger exercises (though later, as a teacher himself, he placed great reliance on such systematic foundation). His father noted that 'the mechanism of playing took you little time, and your mind rather than your fingers were busy. If others spent whole days struggling with the keyboard you rarely spent a whole hour at it...'

Within a short while of starting with Żywny, Chopin began to play in public, and by early 1818 was already being described in the diary of one Aleksandra Tańska-Hoffmanowa as 'Mozart's successor'. As a prodigy of only seven he enjoyed wide popularity, but wasn't vain. After his first major concert, at the Radziwiłł Palace on 24 February 1818, when, billed as 'Schoppin,' he played a Gyrowetz concerto in aid of charity*, his only thoughts, it is said, were not for his talent but for his velvet jacket and collar and what the audience thought of them. He soon came to the attention of several distinguished Polish families, the Zamoyskis, Radziwiłłs and Potockis not least – while yet remaining unspoilt in spite of the burgeoning excitement and praise. Meanwhile, his father ensured that his general education wasn't neglected – until the age of thirteen Chopin studied at home under his supervision.

In the first months of lessons with Żywny, Chopin began to compose, and in November 1817 a short Polonaise in G minor – in the style of Prince Ogiński – was published, dedicated to Wiktoria Skarbek (the Countess's cousin, a witness at his birth). 'The composer of this Polish dance [is] a musical genius,' reported the *Pamiętnik Warszawski* in January 1818: 'not only does he play the most difficult pieces on the pianoforte, with the greatest ease and exceptional taste, but he is also the composer of several dances and variations, by which musical experts are constantly amazed, above all given the childish age of their writer. Had that young boy been born in Germany or France, he would doubtless have already attracted the attention of all social spheres; may this mention serve as an indication that geniuses also arise on our soil, it is just that the lack of broad publicity conceals them from the public'. 1817 also witnessed a March, which so impressed Grand Duke Constantine that he ordered for it to be scored for military band and performed. Although it

* Other boyhood performances, between the ages of twelve and thirteen, included concertos by Ferdinand Ries and probably also Field (No 5) and Hummel. The Radziwiłł Palace was destroyed in World War II. Reconstructed post-1945, it is today the official residence of the Polish President.

was published no copies seem to have survived, and the original manuscript – written out by his father or Żywny – is lost. Where Chopin's creativity lay wasn't to be doubted: 'my feelings [are expressed] more easily… in notes of music' (6 December 1818). But, like his sister Emilia (and the boy Mendelssohn), he wasn't without other gifts. He enjoyed drawing. And he had a neatly formal way with words – affirmed by this gracefully wreathed name-day greeting to his father, 6 December 1816, aged six:

> When the world declares the festivity of your nameday, my papa, it brings joy to me also, with those wishes; that you may live happily, may not know grievous care, that God may always favour you with the fate you desire — these wishes I express for your sake.

Emilia Chopin (1813-27): anonymous miniature on ivory, c. 1826. 'Dire is man's fate on this world. He suffers, only to suffer more'.

Despite his immersion in music, and his contact from an early age with the poets, writers and artists who used to meet in his father's rooms, Chopin had time for the less *serioso* things of life. He was active and boisterous – rarely if ever the 'frail and sickly' boy novelised by Liszt in his largely erroneous biography of Chopin, published many years later in 1852. He had a lively sense of humour and mimicry, a witty philosophy, and a healthy interest in mixing with his companions, largely the offspring of land-owning hereditary blue-bloods (*szlachta*) – Lyceum boarders under his father's care. His playmates included the children of Countess Zamoyska at the Azure Palace, and the sons of Grand Duke Constantine at the Belweder. As he got older he skated (once cracking his head on the ice), and took pleasure in flirting, sometimes to the consternation of his father. When he was fourteen he wrote to his close school friend, Wilhelm (Wiluś) Kolberg: 'You're not the only one that rides, for I can stick on, too. Don't ask how well, but I can – enough for the horse to go slowly wherever he prefers while I sit fearfully on his back like a monkey on a bear. Until now I haven't had any falls because the horse hasn't thrown me off: but, if ever he should want me to tumble off, I may do it some day' (19 August 1824). A year later he remarks to his parents that his 'health was as good as a faithful dog'. In these years 'little Frycek' was the happiest, most keenly observant, of children.

Chopin, formally uniformed in the school's blue *Ułan* cavalry style, entered the Lyceum, Class IV, in the autumn of 1823 – following a 'starlit' summer at Żelazowa Wola improvising in the open beneath a fig tree. For the next three years music took

Józef Elsner (1769-1854). An Upper Silesian Catholic schooled as a boy by Dominicans and Jesuits. Worthy and prescriptive, he promoted classical values and traditional virtues. Polonaise, rondo and variation were his preferred learning crucibles, Albrechtsberger and Kirnberger with a dash of Fux, his teaching manuals. 'Everything should advance toward one goal... each goal must appear as belonging to such totality... all beauty lies in the union of totality and multiplicity'. Chopin was his favourite pupil.

second place. Latin and Greek were good but, for all his efforts, his spelling refused to improve: to the end of his life he mis-spelt foreign words. During the long hot summers of Central Europe, he would go for his holidays to the country estates of his friends. Here, away from Warsaw, he came under the influence of Polish/Jewish peasants and their music-making. This is colourfully revealed in the columns of a 'newspaper' which he and Emilia wrote during summer 1824, the *Szafarnia Courier*, compiled in the manor house of the Dziewanowski family, whose son Dominik (Domuś) attended the Lyceum, lodging with the Chopins. In this spoof 'newspaper' Chopin's awareness of the local flora and fauna, his outlook on life, the revelry, vodka, and shrill out-of-tune singing of the villagers, and his interest in rural music are all communicated vividly. Observing the dance rhythms of the mazurka and other regional steps – which he learned with expert fluency – he found time to experiment and sketch. Back in the salons and ballrooms of the Warsaw aristocracy – the Zamoyskis, the Czartoryskis – the stately, festive polonaise cast other spells, with which he identified and transformed as readily.

1825 was something of a landmark year for Chopin. In the Conservatoire in May and June, 'considered to be the best pianist in Warsaw' (Józefa Kościelska), he demonstrated a newly invented Polish piano-organ, Długosz's *eolipantalion*, impressing with his improvisations and playing of a movement from a piano concerto by the perennially fashionable Moscheles. At the end of May, in the Augsburg Evangelical Church of the Holy Trinity, he was commanded to play Brunner's rival *aeolomelodikon** for Alexander I, the Tsar of Russia and brother of Grand Duke Constantine – who gave him a diamond ring. (Chopin was no stranger to audiences with the illustrious. In the space of only a few years he'd been presented to the Tsar's mother, the Empress Maria Teoderowna, when she visited Warsaw in September 1818; and in November 1819 had played for the great Italian soprano Angelica Catalani, who later gifted him an inscribed gold watch.)

On 2 June the *Kurier Warszawski* announced Brzezina's†
publication of the Rondo in C minor, Op. 1, dedicated to Luiza Linde, the new wife of Chopin's headmaster (she nineteen, he fifty-three). Introduced on the *eolipantalion* eight days later, this remarkably advanced piece helped consolidate the impression made before the Tsar, and the warm praise of the influential Prince Radziwiłł, together with the appreciation of a leading German music magazine, the Leipzig *Allgemeine musikalische Zeitung*, must have greatly pleased the Chopin household. (Since leaving Żywny in 1822, he'd been taking private lessons with Józef Elsner, Director of the new Warsaw Conservatoire.)

The summer was spent at Szafarnia, with a trip to medieval, fortified Toruń (then across the border in Prussia), the birthplace of Chopin's godfather, Fryderyk Skarbek, famous for Copernicus and gingerbread ('nothing outshines the cakes!'), and a harvest festival at nearby Obrowo. 'From afar the sound of choirs of false descants, comprising now women gaggling through their noses, now girls a semitone higher mercilessly squawking the greater part of their heads off, to the accompaniment of a single violin, and that with three strings, which emitted its alto voice from the back after each verse that was sung' (24 August).

Chopin's final year at the Lyceum concentrated on general subjects: his father was anxious that he should acquit himself well in classics and mathematics. During this academic year Chopin was made organist of the school ('the most important person in the whole Lyceum, after his reverence the priest!' he wrote in November), and though he never composed for the organ, it was an instrument that left its influence. He frequently accompanied

* Another Brunner invention, the *choralion*, was demonstrated in December 1826.

† Antoni Brzezina ran a local music shop, one of Chopin's regular haunts along with Fryderyk Buchholtz's prized piano factory and rehearsal room (he played a Buchholtz at home).

Chopin's birthplace, the porch having been added later.

and extemporised at the Church of the Nuns of the Visitation, often in a most daring fashion, and several of his contemporaries left warm accounts of his playing. After leaving Poland, however, he seldom touched the instrument.

Christmas that year was spent with Countess Skarbek and Ludwika in the snowy environs of Żelazowa Wola. Back in Warsaw in 1826 his preparations for the summer examinations left little time for either correspondence or music. But in the late spring he noted with some regret that 'my Botanical Gardens [at Kazimierz Palace, home of the Lyceum and University]... have been beautifully done up by the Commission [as part of a general effort to modernise the city]. There are no more carrots that used to be so nice to eat beside the spring – nor sandwiches, nor arbours, nor salads, nor cabbages nor bad smells: only flower beds in the English style' (15 May).

Chopin had devoted so much time and energy to his general studies that when examination time arrived in July he was exhausted and the strain of sitting the papers proved too much. His health deteriorated. But at the end of the month, hearing he'd shared the class prize, he was able to relax. An effervescent evening at the Opera with Wilhelm Kolberg to hear Rossini's 1817 *La Gazza Ladra* produced a 'farewell' polonaise incorporating one of Kolberg's favourite melodies from Act I, Giannetto's tenor *cavatina* 'Vieni fra queste braccia'.*

* A different 'Rossini' polonaise, on *Il Barbiere di Siviglia*, from October 1825, is lost.

Chopin at the piano: pencil drawing by Eliza Radziwiłłówna, attributed 1829. Dated '1826' in Eliza's album: Chopin visited the Radziwiłł hunting lodge in Antonin for a day in September 1826.

On the 28th he set off by stage-coach for Duszniki-Zdrój [Bad Reinerz], a Silesian mineral spa in the west of Poland, accompanied by his mother, to rendezvous with the Skarbeks and his sisters Ludwika and Emilia. Emilcia, the radiant, laughing girl who 'banished sorrow with jest', was seriously unwell, and no amount of rest or remedy could cure her. 'Spitting blood', she died the following April, from a 'terminal massive gastric haemorrhage' – 'perished in the fourteenth spring of her life, like a flower in which blossomed the beautiful promise of fruit'. Tuberculosis in various forms was all around Chopin. Countess Skarbek died from it on 31 December 1827; his young, close friend Jan Białobłocki from the Lyceum, on 31 March 1828.

The visit to Duszniki-Zdrój proved dull: 'I have been drinking whey and the local waters for two weeks [at the wells by six in the morning at latest], and they say I am looking a little better, but I am [also] said to be getting fat and am as lazy as ever,' he tells Kolberg on 18 August. He had to endure tedious timetables*, and the only real pleasure he obtained was in taking long walks by himself in the hills surrounding the spa: 'Often I am so delighted with the view of these valleys that I hate to come down.'

* Maintained on returning to Warsaw: 'I go to bed at 9. All the teas, *soirées* and balls have gone by the board. I drink emetic water… and feed on oat gruel almost like a horse' (late September). Throughout his life he was intolerant of fatty foods, particularly pork, the consequences of which he learnt to control through dieting.

2. At the Warsaw Conservatoire

'Chopin's variations are constantly running through my head'
Robert Schumann (Florestan)

In September 1826 Chopin enrolled for three years as a student at the Warsaw Conservatoire* with extra University-based lectures timetabled into the curriculum. He studied mainly with Elsner – 'precisely six hours of counterpoint a week'. While Elsner, himself a successful if academically inclined composer, was sensitive enough not to impose his will on Chopin, he must, during the first two years, have been confounded by his attempts to grasp classical rigour. For Chopin writing fugues, masses or chamber music, the principles of orchestration, didn't come naturally; he found it hard, too, to channel his energy into prescriptive, stereotyped musical forms and procedures. He wanted to get on with *his* kind of music, writing for *his* instrument. Anything else produced uncertain results – witness the First Piano Sonata, music of a provincial apprenticeship, from between the deaths of Beethoven and Schubert, inscribed to Elsner. Demonstrably the only moments of originality here are when he seeks to depart from the requirements mapped out by his teacher (principally the 5/4 slow movement). Of no consolation on a day-to-day basis was the irony that many of the practices Chopin was expected or advised to follow were predominantly the outcome of schoolroom 'rules' foreign to the gospel of Bach and Mozart he'd worshipped since a boy.

Left to himself Chopin could invent and write as he pleased. Nobody restricted his natural curiosity, or questioned his methods. Among his more unusual efforts, neatly combining personal licence with professorial formula, was the *Rondo à la Mazur*, Op. 5. Arrestingly, this uses the sharpened fourth degree characteristic of the Lydian mode (that is to say, B natural – not B flat – in the scale of F major), typical of certain Polish field tunes. In later years Chopin was to provocatively integrate such traits within his vocabulary.

From 1827 dates his first Nocturne (the perennial E minor, Op. 72 No. 1), a form he was to make uniquely his own, adapting it from the examples of John Field, the pianistically influential

* Founded in 1810 as a school for singers and theatre actors. In 1821 it became the Institute of Music and Declamation, affiliated with the University of Warsaw, the Main or High School branch of which, directed by Elsner, being responsible for theory and composition. Following the dissolution of the University by the Russians after the November 1830 Uprising (see Chapter 4), it was revived in 1861 as the Institute of Music, changing its name to the Warsaw Conservatoire in 1918. In 1946 it became the Higher State School of Music, then in 1979 the Fryderyk Chopin Music Academy. Since 2008 it has been known as the Fryderyk Chopin University of Music.

John Field (1782–1837): steel engraving attributed to Carl Mayer. Wandering dreamer more than bravura showman, old-fashioned to many, socially and culturally rough-edged, over-shadowed by the rising star of Mendelssohn and the avangardists across the Channel, Protestant Irish exile, reclusive Russian 'prince'.

Dublin-born London apprentice of Clementi who lived in Moscow. Liszt, in an edition of Field's nocturnes published in Paris in 1859, voiced an admiration felt universally:

> The charm which I have always found in these pieces, with their wealth of melody and refinement of harmony, goes back to the years of my earliest childhood. Long before I dreamed of ever meeting their creator, I had given myself up for hours at a time to the soothing influences of the visions flowing from the gentle intoxication of this music.

Later in the same essay Chopin's development of the genre is summarised in words of resonantly Romantic exuberance:

> Even under the names of Nocturnes, we have seen the shy, serenely tender emotions which Field charged them to interpret, supplanted by strange and foreign effects. Only one genius possessed himself of this style, lending to it all

the movement and ardour of which it was susceptible, yet preserving all its tenderness and the poising flight of its aspirations. Filling the entire scope of elegiac sentiment, and colouring his reveries with the profound sadness for which Youth found some chords of so dolorous vibration, Chopin, in his poetic Nocturnes, sang not only the harmonies which are the source of our most ineffable delights, but likewise the restless, agitating bewilderment to which they often give rise. His flight is loftier, though his wing be more wounded: and his very suaveness grows heart-rendering, so thinly does it veil his despairful anguish. We may never hope to surpass—which, in the arts, means to equal—that pre-eminence of inspiration and form with which he endowed all the pieces he published under this title. Their closer kinship to sorrow than those of Field renders them the more strongly marked; their poetry is more sombre and fascinating; they ravish us more, but are less reposeful, and thus permit us to return with pleasure to those pearly shells that open, far from the tempests and the immensities of the Ocean, beside some murmuring spring shaded by the palms of a happy oasis which makes us forget even the existence of the desert *.

Most important of Chopin's early works was the set of expression-cum-character-cum-virtuoso Variations on *Là ci darem la mano* from Mozart's opera *Don Giovanni,* for piano and orchestra, written as a composition exercise during the summer of 1827. The theme Chopin used (he may have seen Kurpiński's Warsaw production of the opera in 1822) was a favourite one with composers of the *brillante* school – the Act I duet between the Don and Zerlina: 'There we'll take hands and you will whisper "Yes". See, it's close by; let's leave this place, my darling'. Impressed, the twenty-one-year-old Schumann reviewed it in the Leipzig *Allgemeine musikalische Zeitung* (7 December 1831) 'Off with your hats, gentlemen – a genius… I bend before Chopin's spontaneous genius, his lofty aim, his mastership!' Famous words. It was Chopin's first serious appreciation as a composer.

Despite spiralling political tensions, Warsaw in the 1820s was an artistically 'vibrant' place – 'home to an opera house, various smaller theatres, one of the earliest modern conservatories in Europe, several societies which organized concerts, musically

* Translated Theodore Baker.

Gioachino Rossini (1792–1868): anonymous etching, 1820. Man of the world, gourmand, recluse. 'Eating, loving, singing and digesting, truthfully, are the four acts of the comic opera that is life, and they pass like bubbles from a bottle of champagne. Whoever lets them break without having enjoyed them is a complete fool'.

* Halina Goldberg, 'Chopin in Warsaw's Salons', *Polish Music Journal*, Vol. 2/i-ii, 1999.

active churches, and a spirited salon life. For a short time it even had a weekly paper devoted exclusively to music. The instrument-building industry produced ever-growing numbers of pianos, and music printers issued large quantities of fashionable salon favourites: popular songs, dances, piano arrangements, rondos, variations, and fantasies' *. At the National Theatre, under Kurpiński and Elsner, one could join the world and have one's fill of Rossini – together with the latest French, German and local fare. On the concert stage the brightest, most brilliant stars of the virtuoso high-wire spun their magic. One highlight in the spring of 1828 was a visit by the composer, pianist and teacher Hummel, an opportunity Chopin didn't miss. Hummel's

music and style of playing, combining classical simplicity with romantic intensity and dexterity of fingerwork, was inspirational, anticipating features in Chopin's own work. Chopin made the *maestro's* acquaintance – provably the first widely important composer of the period with whom he came into personal contact.

In September 1828, after the holidays, a colleague of his father's needed to attend a zoological conference in Berlin and invited Chopin to accompany him. Berlin, the capital of Prussia under Friedrich Wilhelm III, was the centre of a flourishing musical life. Ever since the end of the 17th century, from the time of the Electors of Brandenburg, opera, in particular, was held in high esteem. Berlin in the late 18th century witnessed performances of such seminal masterworks as Mozart's *Seraglio*, *Le Nozze di Figaro* and *Don Giovanni*, while in June 1821, after a long and bitter struggle against the dominance of imported Italian opera (popular with the king), the German national school triumphed with the premiere of Weber's *Der Freischütz* at the new Königliches Schauspielhaus.

Chopin may have been out of his comfort zone in the company of scientists and learned elders – whom he frequently caricatured in his letters – but was happy to immerse himself in

Above: Berlin 'nature scholars': crayon caricatures by Chopin, September 1828.

Right: Niccolò Paganini (1782–1840): pencil drawing by Ingres, 1819. 'Whereas in public concerts this great virtuoso astonishes with fluency, overcoming extraordinary difficulties and bringing hitherto unknown sounds out of the instrument, in [salon] quartets a new [experience], almost one of ecstasy, intoxicates the listener's senses... he amazes and touches' - *Kurier Warszawski,* 18 July 1829.

Overleaf: Berlin, Unter den Linden, the grandest boulevard of 19th century Berlin: detail from a painting by Wilhelm Brücke, 1842.

the abundance of new 'celebrity' music which he heard. Handel's *Ode for St. Cecilia's Day* for soloists, chorus and orchestra made a profound impression: he wrote to his family on 20 September that it 'is nearer to the ideal that I have formed of great music'. His passion for the human voice, be it in opera, oratorio or song, his physical attraction to singers, never left him.

One day Chopin found himself in the presence of the multi-talented Mendelssohn – but 'I felt shy about introducing myself'. Though Mendelssohn was scarcely a year older he was more a man of the world, with the overture *A Midsummer Night's Dream,* the Octet, and well over a dozen symphonies and concertos already to his credit. The cosmopolitan atmosphere of Mendelssohn's world – Germany, Switzerland, France – together with his wealthy family's celebrated Sunday morning concerts in their mansion on the Leipziger Strasse combined to give him a confidence Chopin could only yet aspire to.

1828 focussed on course-work for the Conservatoire. By now

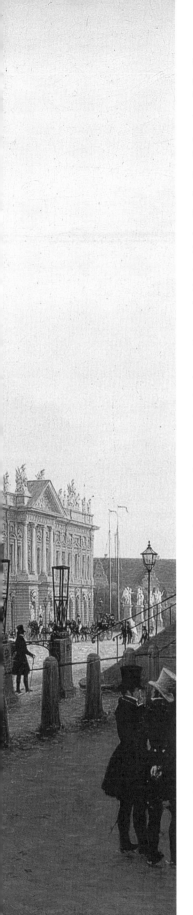

Chopin was seeking to find compromises between his own ideas and the didactic brief of his professors. He composed a Piano Trio, Op. 8, dedicated to Prince Antoni Radziwiłł. And wrote two new works for piano and orchestra: the *Grand Fantasia on Polish Airs*, Op. 13, and the *Krakoviak*, 'Grand Concert Rondo', Op. 14. The *krakoviak* was a Polish dance in duple metre, originating in the Kraków region of southern Poland, in those days a 'Free, Independent, and Strictly Neutral City' republic, independent of Warsaw, controlled by Russia, Prussia and Austria. Contrasting the mazurka and polonaise, the *krakoviak* influenced Chopin to a lesser extent. But in this work his absorption of dance rhythms, and the lyric poetry that blossoms from the opening mists of orchestral sound and piano phrases voiced at the double-octave, adds up to a lingering evocation of atmospheric colour. The *Krakoviak* endures among the most carefully finished of his student ventures.

In the spring of 1829, conscious that the Conservatoire years were drawing to a close, Chopin's family decided that nothing would be gained by keeping him in Warsaw. On 13 April his father, on the basis of his son's reputation, potential promise, and standing with the Establishment, sent a petition to the Minister of Religion and Public Education in which funding was requested with a view to supporting Chopin on his intended travels through Europe, 'especially Germany, Italy and France, so as to form himself upon the best models'. Such a Grand Tour was a normal enough expectation for the period. The application was refused, to the dismay of everyone, Elsner included: 'public funds should not be ~~wasted~~ [*sic*] assigned for the encouragement of this type of artist' (20 June).

On 24 May, in the Royal Castle, Nikolai I, Tsar of Russia in succession to Alexander I, crowned himself King of Poland – to a polite reception from a Warsaw public with little to celebrate. Chopin's attention was taken up by events more immediate to his interests: the visit of Niccolò Paganini (23 May–14 July). Paganini's technical wizardry and 'devilish' mastery of the violin had long dazzled the musical stages of Europe. Only the previous year he'd given concerts in Vienna which had taken that city, so critical in its judgement, by storm. Clothes 'in the style of Paganini' appeared in shop windows, and the Austrian Emperor, Franz I, created him 'Virtuoso of the Court'. Paganini exerted wide influence on 19th century musicians: Liszt, Schumann and Brahms were unanimous in their devotion. Chopin, conscious, like Liszt, of radical techniques and

Tobias Haslinger (1787–1842),
Viennese publisher whose catalogue
ranged from Spohr to Johann Strauss
Senior, Clementi to Moscheles:
watercolour by Josef Kriehuber, 1832.

innovative sonorities in Paganini's playing, jotted down a little
Souvenir de Paganini, based on the Neapolitan air *O mamma,
mamma cara* (*The Carnival of Venice*), then newly set by the
great man for violin and orchestra. Paganini's influence was
to emerge most clearly, however, in the first set of Studies,
Op. 10, which Chopin began to sketch that autumn.

In July Chopin sat his final examinations. For all his
waywardness and apparent disinterest in the curriculum,
he passed without difficulty. When he walked out of the
Conservatoire for the last time, his years of study behind him, he
carried a glowing commendation from Elsner, who drew attention
in his report to Chopin's 'outstanding abilities [and] musical
genius' – valued words from so severe and demanding a seer.

3. Travels and Farewell to Poland

'The native melody is like the climate of the mother country'

Stefan Witwicki

Despite Chopin's family failing to obtain a grant from the Ministry, they were still insistent, despite limited resources, that he should go abroad, aware that Berlin the previous year had opened up new horizons for him. Finishing the Conservatoire on 20 July, he left Warsaw almost immediately. His destination was Vienna, which, after Paris, was the most important musical centre of the Western world. Vienna's legacy and life was vast and varied. On the one hand, countless composers and hacks penned popular salon music and dances. On the other, the spirit of Haydn, Mozart and Beethoven loomed over everything. Beethoven, indeed, had only been dead two years.

Journeying by diligence (four horse stage-coach) through Kraków, and climbing the passes of the picturesque but hazardous highlands of eastern Moravia, dust by day, rain by night, Chopin arrived in Vienna on 31 July 1829. Within the week he'd been to three operas, including Rossini's *La Cenerentola*. But there was a more serious purpose to his visit. The influential Austrian music publisher, Tobias Haslinger – whose publications included some of Beethoven's most important works as well as a few by Schubert – had already been sent manuscripts of Chopin's First Sonata, and the *Là ci darem* Variations, but, a shrewd businessman, was reluctant to publish music by a new and unknown composer. He changed his mind on reading a praiseworthy letter from Elsner, and hearing Chopin play. He offered to publish the Variations – without payment – on condition that Chopin introduce them at a public concert. Chopin was unprepared for this. It was one thing to visit Vienna on holiday and play privately, quite another to appear before a critical public, particularly when so much depended on the outcome. He was, as usual, careless about his practice, and justifiably nervous, but the enthusiasm of so many patrons in Vienna, the enticement of a fine Graf *Hammerflügel* to play, and the loan of the Kärntnertortheater*, persuaded him. On 11 August, at 7pm, 'I made my entry into the world'. Following Beethoven's *Prometheus* overture, with 'a painted young man

* Where Beethoven's Ninth Symphony, the 1814 version of *Fidelio*, and Weber's *Euryanthe* had been first performed.

27

Oak-framed Viennese Hammerflügel by Conrad Graf, c. 1825.

beside me who turned the pages and prided himself on having rendered the same service to Moscheles, Hummel, and Herz,' he presented *Là ci darem*. 'In his playing,' reviewed the *Wiener Theaterzeitung* (August 20), 'he was like a beautiful young tree that stands free and full of fragrant blossoms and ripening fruits… new figures, new passages, new forms unfolded themselves in the introduction, in the first, second, and fourth variations, and in the concluding metamorphosis of Mozart's theme into a *polacca*'.

In place of the intended *Krakoviak* – abandoned 'at rehearsals because the orchestra accompanied so badly' – he substituted a *freie fantasie*, improvising on Boildieu's 1825 *opéra comique La Dame blanche* and a Polish nuptial song unfamiliar to the Viennese – *Chmiel* (the hop bine), one of the oldest of polonaise tunes, possibly pre-Christian, from western Poland*. The latter reportedly 'electrified the public, as they are not used here to such songs. My spies in the stalls,' he wrote home, 'assure me that people even jumped on their seats!'

Such reservations as there were concerned principally the delicacy of Chopin's projection. 'It is being said everywhere that I played too softly, or rather, too delicately for people used to the piano pounding of the artists here. I expect to find this reproach in the paper, especially as the editor's daughter [Leopoldine Blahetka] thumps frightfully. It doesn't matter: there always must be a *but* somewhere, and I should rather it were that one than have people say I played too loudly' (12 August).

A second concert followed on the 18th. 'If I was well received the first time, it was still better yesterday. The moment I appeared on the stage there were bravos, repeated three times: and there was a larger audience… The second success was better than the first: it goes *crescendo*, that's what I like.' This time everyone got through the *Krakoviak* – Tomasz Nidecki (who'd been a student with Chopin at the Warsaw Conservatoire and was now studying in Vienna on a Polish grant) having tidied up the orchestration and poorly copied parts†. 'I have won over all the professional musicians thanks to my Rondo. From *Kapellmeister* [Franz] Lachner down to the piano-tuner.' 'His style of playing and writing differs greatly from that of other virtuosos; and, indeed chiefly in this, that [perceptive, prescient words] the desire to make good music predominates… over the desire to please' (*Theaterzeitung*, 1 September). 'The lucidity of his interpretation, and his compositions, which bear the stamp of great genius — *variazioni di bravura*, rondo, free fantasia — reveal a virtuoso most liberally endowed by nature, who, without previous blasts

*Traditionally 'sung at midnight, at the wedding ritual of removing the bride's veil. The song associates the relationship of the young couple to that of the hop plant [*humulus lupulus*] and the poles that hold it up' (Maria Pomianowska).

† Nidecki married Elsner's daughter Emilia (by his second marriage). Chopin contributed seventeen pieces to her autograph album, destroyed in World War II.

of trumpets, appears on the horizon like one of the most brilliant meteors' (*Allgemeine musikalische Zeitung*, 18 November). Chopin found himself the talk of the moment. He met a number of influential people, including Czerny (who'd taught Liszt and been a pupil of Beethoven) and Gyrowetz from Bohemia, *Kapellmeister* at the Hoftheater, whose output included operas, concertos and over sixty symphonies. Chopin was also introduced to the Lichnowsky family, originally from Poland. They were among the best known of Viennese patrons, linked closely with Beethoven. Their most illustrious member, Prince Karl, had died in 1814, but Chopin visited Count Moritz 'who couldn't praise me enough... He's the same who was Beethoven's greatest friend' (The *Eroica* piano variations and E minor Sonata were dedicated to him). Almost everyone, with the exception of the 'stony' Germans, complimented Chopin – yet he found few inclined to accept him as a pupil. They frequently riled him with their surprise that anyone could learn so much in a backwater like Warsaw: 'Under Żywny and Elsner the greatest donkey could learn,' he would retort furiously.

Generally, Chopin's Vienna trip had turned out well – 'I am wiser and more experienced by four years'. On 19 August he

Vienna, the Burgtheater, where several of Mozart's operas were premiered, including *Le nozze di Figaro* in 1786, and also Beethoven's First Symphony in 1800.

left after 'tender farewells – really tender' for the next stage of his travels, Prague, capital of the ancient kings of Bohemia but then part of the Austrian Empire under the Habsburgs. 'After many bumpings and joltings [by a small *post-chaise*] we reached Prague yesterday [Friday 21st] at twelve o'clock and went at once to a *table d'hôte* lunch' – at the Modré Hvězdy (Blue Star) off the Old Town Square. Like so many European centres, Prague had a heritage of music going back a thousand years or more, and its audiences were amongst the most discriminating of the time. Their admiration, when roused, could be boundless – to wit Mozart's happy association with the city. Chopin's short visit was uneventful, though he stayed long enough to observe, in a letter to his family, that 'the town is beautiful... when one sees it from the Castle hill: large, ancient and once opulent' (22 August).

Requested to give concerts, Chopin declined, feeling his impression in Vienna had been such that, with their reputation for being scathing and judgemental, the Prague public, who'd thought nothing of dismissing Paganini, might do the same to him – something he wasn't prepared to risk.

Leaving Prague he travelled by road through the Ore Mountains, making for the old city of Dresden via a short sojourn

Prague: engraving by A. H. Payne, 1845. 'The aristocratic beauty of the women of Prague, the way they walk and the way they are attired, so graceful and elegant, reminds me of Dante's *Paradiso*' – Auguste Rodin.

Dresden, a place of 'wide sreets, elegant buildings, and a good store of pretty girls' – Edward Holmes, 1828. 'The Germans are amazed at me and I am amazed at them for finding anything to be amazed about!' - Chopin, 8 August 1829. In February 1945 Allied bombing destroyed 15 square miles of the city.

in Teplice including dinner and rounds of improvisation at the Clary-und-Aldringen *schloss.* Surrounded by old forests, with the Elbe flowing through its centre, Dresden was about the architecture, art collections and libraries that had been greatly enriched during the reigns of the Electors of Saxony in the 17th and 18th centuries. From engravings and paintings of the time, it must have been a memorable sight in Chopin's day – the iconic dome of the Frauenkirche… the tree-shaded river spanned by finely wrought bridges… gondola-like ferries plying their trade or at rest…

One highlight of the Dresden visit was a production of Goethe's *Faust** – a closet drama Beethoven had once thought of adapting as an opera, and which in the 1850s Liszt turned into a programme-symphony focussing on the story's three main characters: Faust, yearning for 'more than earthly meat and drink', the innocent pure Gretchen, and Mephistopheles to whom Faust trades his soul in return for superhuman powers. Following a late 16th century chapbook, the Faust legend had first been dramatised by Marlowe (published posthumously in 1604), based on a wandering German renaissance magician, Johann (Georg) Faust, a student of the black arts denounced by

* First staged that January in Braunschweig (Brunswick), Lower Saxony.

Vienna seen from the Upper Belvedere Palace: painting by Bernardo Bellotto, c.1758-61. 'There is hardly a city in Europe where the drive towards cultural ideals was as passionate as it was in Vienna... Here rode the Nibelungs, here the immortal Pleiades of music shone out over the world... here all the streams of European culture converged' - Stefan Zweig. 'The [full] moon shone exquisitely, the fountains played, a delicious perfume from the open orangery filled the air, in a word: a glorious night and the most delightful place. You can't imagine how beautifully designed is [Dr. Malfatti's countryside] salon: huge windows, thrown open, from which you can see all Vienna; plenty of mirrors; very few lights' - Chopin, 25 June 1831.

the church. A man who filled God-fearing Christians, Martin Luther included, with dread.

The performance Chopin attended, on 26 August, marked Goethe's 80th birthday. Though restricted to an abridgement of Part I of the story, the evening made an immediate impact: 'I have just come back from *Faust*. I had to queue outside the theatre from half-past-four; the play lasted from six to eleven o'clock… It's a terrible phantasy but a great one. Between the acts they played selections from Spohr's opera of the same name [premiered by Weber in Prague in 1816]'. Many a high-Romantic identified dangerously with the Faust legend – without all having the love of a Gretchen to save them. Chopin watched but kept his distance

Leaving Dresden for home Chopin travelled through Wrocław (then the Prussian city of Breslau), historical capital of Silesia, the flat terrain of the land contrasting with the mountainous landscape of Bohemia and Saxony. He arrived in Warsaw on 12 September, and the remainder of the year was spent making chamber music every Friday at the home of Joseph Kessler, a composer, pianist and teacher to whom he later dedicated the Leipzig edition of the Op. 28 *Préludes* (July

Johann Wolfgang von Goethe (1749-1832). 'A talent can be cultivated in tranquility; a character only in the rushing stream of life' - *Torquato Tasso*, 1790.

1839). On these occasions he wasn't under the strain of public concert-giving, and could comfortably explore the pages of works like Spohr's Octet or Beethoven's *Archduke* Piano Trio, late C sharp minor String Quartet and early A flat Sonata, Op. 26*, all of which left a deep and lasting impression. 'I have not heard something so great for a long time.' By now he was enough of an individual to have an opinion of his own, never mind that Beethoven's music, in particular, was unfashionable with Varsovians. Notwithstanding, such discerning sensibility, encouraged at a developmental stage by Żywny, had yet to translate into self-expression – compositionally, the precedent, prettiness and pianism of in-demand composers like Hummel, Moscheles and Kalkbrenner continued foreseeably to be the more attractive terrain to cultivate.

During this period Chopin began his most important composition to date, the Concerto in F minor, completed the following spring (known as No. 2 since it was published after the later E minor). In contrast to earlier works, the emotional character of the Moscheles-inflexioned F minor and such smaller pieces as the *Lento con gran espressione* Nocturne written for Ludwika (using themes from the concerto), in particular

* He taught the A flat to the end of his life, and in one celebrated instance – the *marche funèbre* of the Second Sonata, Op. 35 – borrowed the drum-rolls of its (likewise third-placed) funeral march movement.

Right: Wrocław [Breslau] University.

Below: Konstancja Gładkowska (1810-89), *c.* 1845. Chopin's second love, partially reciprocated, finally unrequited. She went blind in her thirties. 'Foreigners can better reward and appreciate you,/But they cannot love you more than we', November 1830.

the poetry and passion beneath the aristocratic veneer, point to new tensions. Chopin's letters to his brother-in-spirit Titus Woyciechowski (dedicatee of the *Là ci darem* Variations) intimate why. His life is in a state of flux… there are plans to travel and study, 'I shall not stay in Warsaw'… he is in love* (3 October):

> O, perhaps unfortunately, I already have my ideal, whom I have served faithfully, though silently, for half a year, of whom I dream, to thoughts of whom the *adagio* of my concerto belongs, and who this morning inspired the little waltz [Op. 70 No. 3, in D flat major] I am sending you… You wouldn't believe how dreary I find Warsaw now. If it weren't for the family making it a little more cheerful, I wouldn't stay. But how dismal it is to have no one to go to in the morning to share one's griefs and joys; how hateful when something weighs on you and there's nowhere to lay it down. You know to what I refer. I often tell my pianoforte what I want to tell you.

* Not for the first time, 'Mademoiselle la Comtesse' Alexandrine de Moriolles from the Belvedere days having been an earlier distraction – a 'little devil', French, dedicatee of the *Rondo à la Mazur* published in February 1828, who bridged childhood and pubescence and was still tempting him to assignations in the Botanical Gardens as late as 1830.

The young lady who'd momentarily captured Chopin's heart – they met at a student concert, Tuesday 21 April 1829, following Easter – was a pretty blonde soprano, Konstancja Gładkowska, a few months younger than him. During her brief career she became one of the better singers of her time, and like Chopin had enrolled at the Warsaw Conservatoire in 1826. But

Konstancja had many admirers, especially the gallant cavalry officers attached to the local garrison. Ready to fight a duel to the death, they represented insurmountable competition for Chopin, who found it difficult to voice his feelings and sought rather to idealise Konstancja from a distance.

Nicholas probably knew little of his son's anguish but in all likelihood must have been irritated and frustrated by his listless outlook on life. He took matters into his own hands and at the end of October sent him to visit Prince Radziwiłł at his wood-clad hunting lodge in the 'silent' pine and fir forests of Antonin to the south. This diversion temporally put Konstancja out of Chopin's thoughts, at least on the surface. He liked the Prince's two young daughters, writing to Titus on 14 November: 'So far as my temporary personal pleasure went, I would have stopped [here] till they turned me out, but my affairs, particularly my unfinished concerto, which is waiting impatiently for the completion of the finale, spurred me on to abandon [this] paradise. There were two Eves in it: young princesses, very kind and friendly, musical, sensitive creatures'. He gave a few lessons to one of them, Wanda: 'She is quite young: seventeen and pretty; really it was a joy to guide her delicate fingers'. (Antoni Radziwiłł, the Prussian-appointed governor of the Grand Duchy of Posen, whose Berlin palace later became Bismarck's Reich Chancellery, was an amateur composer and cellist. Chopin admired music he'd written for Goethe's *Faust* – 'he's a whole-hearted Gluckist' – even addressing certain of its technical and staging details in correspondence with Titus.)

Back in Warsaw Chopin continued work on the F minor Concerto, his feelings for Konstancja hightened through accompanying for her at the Conservatoire, and he began to heed the demands of local audiences. He'd already given two successful concerts in Vienna, and the Warsaw press voiced the mood of the public when they wrote: 'Does not Mr. Chopin's talent belong to his country? Does he think that Poland is incapable of appreciating him? Mr. Chopin's works bear unquestionably the stamp of genius.' A profile appearance could be put off no longer. On 3 March 1830 a trial run was arranged in the drawing room of the Chopin household at Krasiński Palace with a select private audience. Karol Kurpiński, who with Elsner was manager of the Warsaw Opera as well as author of numerous (Italianate) operas, directed, and Chopin played his *Fantasia on Polish Airs* (incorporating one of Kurpiński's own melodies) and the F minor. The occasion was a success. On 17

Chopin: pencil drawing by Eliza Radziwiłłówna, 7 November 1829. 'Very much like me, I am told'. 'The striking feature about his face was the lack of growth of facial hair and beard... noted by himself [and others]... "I have one side-whisker - the other won't simply grow"' - J. A. Kuzemko.

March Chopin made his official adult *début* at the National Theatre, Krasiński Square, playing the same works.

The concert was sold out three days beforehand, and the audience was approving. One of them, moved by the experience and oblivious of time – eleven o'clock at night – wrote enthusiastically:

> I have just returned from the concert by Chopin, that artist whom I heard playing when he was seven, when he was still a hope for the future. How beautifully he plays today! What fluency What evenness!... his music is full of expressive feeling and song, and puts the listener into a state of subtle rapture, bringing back to his memory all the happy moments he has known.

Chopin wasn't satisfied, however, feeling his real success came with a subsequent performance, given a few days later on the 22nd in response to popular demand. He replaced the *Fantastia* with the *Krakoviak*, and used a more powerfully toned Viennese piano which projected the sound better than his own quiet instrument. Reviewing the *col legno* folk-finale Concerto, Maurycy Mochnacki compared it 'to the life of an honest man, no ambiguity, falsity, exaggeration… the whole is subordinated to the genius of music, which it breathes and exhales… It is always new, fresh, in a word inspired' (*Kurier Polski*, 24 March).

Within a month, faithful to his promise, Haslinger published the *Là ci darem* Variations in Vienna, doing much to promote Chopin's name among Austrian and German musicians. By now work was well under way on the 'warhorse' E minor Concerto (No. 1), a bigger-gestured score more obviously 'public' than the F minor while still sharing common expressive ground. Konstancja lingers wraith-like across the muted slow movement, vanishing in a mirror of splintered crystal. 'It is not meant to be loud – it's more of a romance, quiet, melancholic; it should give the impression of gazing tenderly at a place which brings to mind a thousand dear memories. It is a sort of meditation in beautiful spring weather but by moonlight' (to Titus, 15 May).

During the Tsar's opening of the Polish Sejm (Diet, Parliment) in May and June, a host of brilliant artists visited Warsaw. Chopin relished them all, not least the illustrious German Henrietta Sontag, the original soprano of Beethoven's Ninth and *Missa Solemnis*, none of whose eight concerts he missed: 'her *diminuendi* are *non plus ultra*, her *portamenti* are lovely, her ascending chromatic scales are exquisite'. On 24 July – following a few days with Titus on the isolated Woyciechowski flatland estate at Poturzyn (Polish-Ukrainian 'frontier country), 'taking the local folk songs in his heart' – he attended Konstancja's opera *début* in Paer's 1809 *Agnese*, spotting qualities either missed or ravaged by the critics. Splendid 'tragic acting', phrasing to delight, 'gorgeous shading'.

In August the family went to their old home at Żelazowa Wola, but within weeks plans were afoot for Chopin to leave Poland on fresh travels in search of new glories. The unsettled political climate, on the other hand, altered many of his intentions. On September 22nd he wrote to Titus, 'My dearest Life!':

My father did not wish me to travel, a few weeks ago, on account of the disturbances which are starting all over Germany: not counting the Rhine provinces, the Saxons—who already have another king [Anton the Kind] —Brunswick, Cassel, Darmstadt and so on. We heard, too, that in Vienna some thousands of people had begun to become sulky about the flour. I don't know what was wrong with the flour, but I know there was something. In the Tyrol, also, there have been arguments. The Italians do nothing but boil over... I have not yet tried for my [Russian authorised] passport, but people tell me that I can get one only to Austria and Prussia; no use to think of Italy and France. And I know that several persons have been refused passports altogether, but that would doubtless not happen to me. So I shall probably go within the next few weeks through Kraków to Vienna, for people there have now refreshed their memory of me [through publication of the Variations] and I must take advantage of that.

Chopin finalised the E minor by the end of August, giving the first public performance at the National Theatre on Monday 11 October 1830 at what was to be his farewell Warsaw concert. Conducted by Carlo Soliva ('a tricky [Swiss] Italian'), it was the centrepiece of the programme, together with the *Polish Fantasia*. 'I was not a bit, not a bit nervous,' he wrote to Titus the day after, 'and played the way I play when I'm alone, and it went well.' Konstancja, 'dressed in white, with roses in her hair,' added to the completeness of the evening, singing Rossini. By then, however, their 'platonic' story (Chopin's word), with nowhere to go, had run its course. Later in her life she was surprised to read of his love for her: all she could say was that 'he was temperamental, full of fantasies, and unreliable'... but she kept his letters, only burning them before her death.

In spite of Chopin's premonition that 'when I leave it will be to forget home forever: I feel that I am leaving home only to die', a day for departure had to be chosen. He left Warsaw, his family and Konstancja – with whom he exchanged rings – on 2 November 1830, a Tuesday. On the outskirts of the city, Elsner conducted a cantata he'd written for the occasion. As the stage-coach trundled south-westwards towards Vienna, Chopin, in a sense tracing in reverse the footsteps of his father before him, said goodbye to his native soil and prepared to face the reality of life on the troubled stage of Europe.

4. New Horizons

'His inspirations were powerful, fantastic, impulsive'

Franz Liszt

Chopin: oil portrait by Ambroży Mieroszewski, 1829. 'Throughout his Warsaw years Chopin lived with the clamour for independence ringing in his ears' - Jim Samson.

With Chopin's original plans for his journey to Vienna altered, the route taken finally, with Titus joining two days later, followed the one on his return to Warsaw from Vienna in 1829. In Wrocław he played the rondo of the E minor Concerto at a private gathering: one diversion of this centred around a local amateur pianist who, after hearing Chopin play, backed out of his own commitments to perform.

The next stop was Dresden, where Chopin renewed his friendship with the German composer August Klengel, a former pupil of Clementi and official organist to the Dresden Court, whom he'd first met in Prague in August 1829: 'I respect him greatly... I like to talk with him because one can really learn something.' Klengel wanted Chopin to give a concert, 'but about that I am deaf. I have no time to lose, and Dresden will give me neither fame nor money' (letter to his family, 14 November). Nevertheless he played a concerto for Klengel privately: 'It reminded him of Field's playing, that I have a rare touch, that although he had heard much about me, he had never expected to find me such a virtuoso. It was not idle compliment: he told me that he hates to flatter anyone or force himself to praise them' (21 November).

After passing through Prague, Chopin and Titus arrived in Vienna on 23 November. If his earlier visit had been encouraging, Chopin this time encountered a cool reserve when it came to giving concerts or promoting his compositions. On a social level he was still made welcome, but social niceties were not going to boost his funds. Haslinger, unprepared to run his business at a loss, politely refused to take on any more of his music. In those days Viennese *bon-bon* audiences, taking their cue from the monarchy, preferred the waltzes of the elder Strauss or Joseph Lanner, and had an insatiable appetite for fantasias and *potpourris* on popular operatic tunes, however cheaply turned out. Chopin laments to Elsner that 'here waltzes are called works!', while in another letter he remarks on 'the corrupt

The Paradeplatz in Vienna, a popular walking spot: engraving by Leopold Beyer, 1805.

taste of the Viennese public'. For too many Austrian publishers, aware that easy gratification spelt money, the budding originality and perfume of an unknown twenty-year old's work was not a tenable proposition, promising indifferent sales at best.

Neither was the delicate, unspectacular quality of his piano playing a commercial proposition. One impresario told Chopin that he could not advise him to become a soloist 'for there are so many good pianists here that one needs a great reputation to gain anything'.

In letters home, not wishing to worry his family, Chopin makes a pretext of enjoying himself. He attends *soirées* and lavish balls given by the nobility and, with Titus, finds lodgings in one of the main streets of Vienna, the Kohlmarkt: 'three rooms, on the third floor, it's true, but delightful, splendid, elegantly furnished'. By day the street bustled noisily with people and the cobblestones rang with the sound of horses' hooves and the rattle of carriages. By night the tall houses – with their long windows and carved masonry over silent shops or stables – were illuminated by gas lamps (a novel innovation adopted in 1818),

A masked ball in the Redoutensaal, the Hofburg Palace, Vienna: engraving by J. Schütz, c.1800.

becoming a shadowy world of fantasy and fairy tale.

On the Wednesday before Christmas (22 December) Chopin wrote saying that he now had rooms on the *fourth* floor: 'How nice it is... A roof opposite me and pigmies down below. I am higher than they! The best moment is when, having finished playing on Graf's dull piano, I go to bed with your letters in my hand. Then, even in sleep, I see only you!... I don't want to say goodbye to you, I should like to keep on writing.' He allows just a little anxiety to mar the cheerful pose: 'In one way I am glad to be here, but in another!'

A different Chopin – depressed, lonely, and uncertain of his future – emerges in letters to his friends, particularly Jan Matuszyński, to whom he unburdened his frustrations freely. On hearing that Warsaw had revolted against the Tsar, his mood reached a fever point of melancholic despondency. He feared Russian reprisals and worried about his family and his home, about everything he'd ever known and loved.

This revolt was yet another disturbance in a Europe seething with discontent, each country anxious to assert its national identity and be free of foreign overlords. It stemmed more immediately from reports of the Paris revolution that July. Discontented army factions promptly planned an overthrow of the government. But the attempt was abortive and it was not until 29 November, a few weeks after Chopin left Warsaw, that Poland found itself strong enough to mount an uprising – which Titus joined as soon as he heard the news in Vienna, leaving a disconsolate Chopin behind. A 'National Revolution' was declared at a meeting of the Sejm on 13 December 1830, with Prince Adam Czartoryski appointed President of the new National Government just over six weeks later (29 January). The Russians declared this defiance to be an 'odious crime' and an army, 115,000 strong, marched towards Lithuania to crush the insurrection, the first engagement of the ensuing Russo-Polish War taking place on 14 February 1831 at the Battle of Stoczek.

On Christmas Day 1830 Chopin wrote a long letter to Jan, full of unbridled changes of mood – from the depths of depression to carefree comments on his surroundings. Vienna

The Kohlmarkt, Vienna: tinted engraving by Leopold Beyer. Chopin lived at No. 9, the headquarters of the music publishers Artaria.

St. Stephen's Cathedral, Vienna. Christmas Day 1830: 'My health is bad. I am gay on the outside, especially among my own (I count Poles my own), but inside something gnaws at me; some foreboding, disquiet, a dream or sleeplessness – longing – indifference – a desire for life, the next instant a desire for death; some kind of sweet peace, a sort of numbness, an unconsciousness of mind, sometimes a rigorous memory, torments me. My mind is sour, bitter, salty, some hideous jumble of feelings shakes me!'

was a city suddenly hostile towards the Poles – despite Austria maintaining a neutral stand in the Russo-Polish conflict – and Chopin found himself a lone wolf, with few people to turn to, and still fewer pleasures of any meaning. It was his first Christmas away from his family. His letter opens with a wistful contradiction of the Yuletide spirit:

> Today I am sitting alone, in a dressing-gown, gnawing my ring and writing. If it were not that I should be a burden on my father, I would come back. I curse the day I left. I am up to the neck in evening parties, concerts and dances, but they bore me to death; everything is so terribly gloomy and depressing for me here. I have to dress and get ready to go out: in company I must appear calm, and then when I come home I let myself go on the piano. The other part [of your letter] has grieved me deeply. Is there really not even a little change? Did

she [Konstancja] not fall ill? I could easily believe such
a thing about so sensitive a creature... Is it perhaps the
terror of the 29th? May God forbid that it should be my
fault! Calm her, say that so long as my strength lasts—
that till death—that even after death, my ashes will
strew themselves at her feet.

Later he describes Midnight Service in St. Stephen's, in the
centre of the walled city, overlooking the curving waters of the
Danube flowing eastwards towards the Black Sea in the eye of
the rising sun:

When I entered there was no one there. Not to hear the
Mass, but just to look at the huge building at that hour.
I got into the darkest corner at the foot of a Gothic pillar.
I can't describe the greatness, the magnificence of those
huge arches. It was quiet; now and then the footsteps of
a sacristan, lighting candles at the back of the sanctuary,
would break into my lethargy. A coffin behind me, a
coffin under me—only the coffin above me was lacking...
I have never felt my loneliness so clearly.

A few paragraphs later he asks:

Shall I go to Paris? The people here advise me to wait.
Shall I come back to Poland? Shall I stay here? Shall I put
an end to myself? Shall I stop writing to you? Advise me
what to do.

He spent several days writing this letter. By the end, his
gloominess lightening temporarily, he gives a pen sketch of
everyday life:

My room is big and comfortable, with three windows,
the bed opposite the windows; a splendid *pantaléon**
on the right side, a sofa on the left, mirrors between the
windows; in the middle, a fine, big, round mahogany
table; a polished parquet floor. It's quiet... so I can
concentrate my thoughts on all of you. In the morning I
am called by an insufferably stupid servant. I get up, they
bring me coffee; I play and mostly have a cold breakfast.
About 9 comes the *maître* for the German language. After
that I usually play... all this in a dressing-gown until

* Jean-Jacques Eigeldinger points
out that 'from Chopin's pen, in his
Polish letters, the word *pantalion*
seems simply to designate a grand
piano (as opposed to a square
piano)'. By the end of the 18th
century the term was used by
German speakers to describe the
reverse.

noon. After that comes a very worthy German… who works in the prison, and if the weather is fine we go for a walk on the *glacis* round the town, after which I go to dinner if I am invited anywhere. If not we go together to the place frequented by the entire academic youth: that is Zur Boemische Köchlin. After dinner, black coffee is drunk in the best *kaffeehaus*—that is the custom here. Then I pay visits, return home at dusk, curl my hair, change my shoes, and go out for the evening; about 10, 11 or sometimes 12—never later—I come back, play, weep, look, laugh, go to bed, put the light out, and always dream about some of you.

On 1 January he writes again to Jan, his narrative back to despair, the child of old facing the roads of manhood:

What are my friends doing? I live with you all, I would die for you, for all of you. Why am I so alone? Is it only you who can be together at so fearful a moment?... Today is New Year—how sadly I begin it! Perhaps I shall not end it. Embrace me. You are going to the war. Come back a colonel. Good luck to you all. Why can't I beat the drum!

To this period – 'according to tradition, not supported in evidence' (Mieczysław Tomaszewski) – belong purportedly the First Scherzo – in which a Polish Christmas carol is introduced, veiled in the surrounding harmonies of the central section; and the dramatic G minor First Ballade – a narrative conception Chopin was to make uniquely his own*. Schumann singled out the G minor among Chopin's 'wildest and most original compositions', writing in one of his letters to Heinrich Dorn that Chopin thought it the best of his (earlier) works. The Scherzo's lullaby heart is a rare example of direct quotation in Chopin's output. The Lancashire composer Alan Rawsthorne recalled how he once 'heard a Polish peasant singing this tune [Lulajże Jezuniu (Sleep, little Jesus)], high up in the Tatra Mountains [between Slovakia and Poland]. The effect was strangely moving in the stillness of the craggy rocks with their patches of snow. His voice came from nowhere in particular, ventriloquially, floating through the mountain air. He sang with abandon, in a quite uninhibited fashion, and with a certain hard, almost ruthless quality that enables the Slavs to get to the heart of their most poignant melodies.'

* On stylistic grounds, and from the paper-type used in the manuscript, the First Ballade, along with the First Scherzo and *Grande valse brillante*, Op. 18 – 'first of the "Paris" waltzes' – is now re-dated to 1833 if not later (Jim Samson, *Chopin: The Four Ballades*, Cambridge 1992).

Homesickness and thoughts of childhood friends on the frontline, prompted several settings of poems by the Polish nationalists, including Stefan Witwicki*. The following lines from Witwicki's *Smutna rzeka* (Sad River) Op. 74 No. 3] resonate. One might almost imagine Chopin staring at the Danube, far from Warsaw and the Vistula, musing in sorrow and memory:

River from foreign regions,
why is your current so murky?
Has the bank fallen in somewhere,
have old snows melted?
The old snows lie on the mountains,
flowers bloom on my banks,
but there, by my spring,
a mother weeps at my spring.
Seven daughters she has brought up,
seven daughters she has buried,
seven daughters in the middle of the garden,
with their heads facing the east.
Now she greets their ghosts,
she asks the children about their comfort,
and she waters their graves
and sings pitiful songs.†

Living in the present needed to replace living off nostalgia. At a matinee on 4 April 'Herr Chopin (piano player)' appeared at the Redoutensaal, offering a solo version of the E minor Concerto. One of ten artists taking part, he made little impact. That he was still in poor mental shape is apparent from his notebook forty-eight hours earlier:

The newspapers and posters have announced my concert. It's to be in two days' time but it is as if there was no such thing: it doesn't seem to concern me. I don't listen to the compliments; they seem to me stupider and stupider. I wish I were dead and yet I would like to see my parents. Her [Konstancja's] image stands before my eyes: I think I don't love her any more, and yet I can't get her out of my head. Everything I have seen abroad till now seems to me old and hateful and just makes me sigh for home, for those blessed moments that I didn't know how to value. What used to seem great, today seems common; what I used to

* Subsequently a friend of Chopin's, and dedicatee of the Op. 41 Mazurkas, Witwicki (1800–47) emigrated to Paris in 1832. He enjoyed the companionship of Mickiewicz until political differences caused a rift.

† Translated Bernard Jacobson.

think common is now incomparable, too great, too high. The people here are not my people: they're kind, but kind from habit; they do everything too respectably, flatly, moderately. I don't even want to think of moderation. I'm puzzled, I'm melancholy, I don't know what to do with myself. I wish I were not alone…

A few weeks later (1 May):

Today it was beautiful on the Prater. Crowds of people with whom I have nothing to do. I admired the foliage, the spring smell, and that innocence of nature which brought back my childhood's feelings. A storm was threatening, so I went indoors—but there was no storm. Only I got melancholy; why? I don't care for even music today. It's late but I'm not sleepy: I don't know what is wrong with me…

Stefan Witwicki (1800-47): bronze medallion by Władysław Oleszczyński, 1841.

The over-riding negativity of his visit, his unhappiness, the superficial charms of his hosts, the lack of recognition – all finally decided Chopin to leave the city. He started making plans for his departure at the end of June. He wanted to go to Paris but since he was legally of Russian nationality this presented difficulties, for Paris was then a refuge for Polish revolutionaries and exiles plotting against the Tsar. Finally he secured a passport to London, with the all-important proviso 'passing through Paris', endorsed further by the French ambassador. That was sufficient. He left on 20 July.

He travelled west along the valley of the Danube to the north of the picturesque Austrian Tyrol, passing first through Salzburg, Mozart's birthplace, and then on to Munich. Here he stopped longer than intended, for money due from his father had not arrived and communications with Warsaw were virtually at a standstill. He took what opportunity this delay offered, and gave a well received concert on 28 August in the Philharmonic Society Hall. The programme included the *Polish Fantasia* and E minor Concerto. Despite a note of caution – 'not distinguished by any special innovation or depth' – it was the first success he'd enjoyed since leaving Warsaw.

A week later, in Stuttgart, came the news of Warsaw's downfall on 6–8 September. Six months of lost battles, out-numbered men, political ineptitude, no foreign support, even the condemnation of the Pope, had stamped Poland's fate. The besieged city panicked, riots broke out, cholera became rampant,

Stuttgart. 'Art is the daughter of Freedom – Friedrich Schiller, *Letters Upon the Aesthetic Education of Man*, 1794.

and the population fought for their lives and liberty. At the mercy of the guns they were forced to surrender. The loss of even the partial independence they'd enjoyed before was completed six months later, in February 1832, when the country became a province of the Russian Empire.

The news left Chopin in shock. In his so-called *Stuttgart Diary* he left frantic, near incoherent fragments:

> The suburbs are destroyed, burned. Jaś [Matuszyński]! Wiluś [Kolberg] probably dead in the trenches. I see Marcel a prisoner! That good fellow Sowiński in the hands of those brutes! Paszkiewicz! Some dog from Mohilov holds the seat of the first monarchs of Europe. Moscow rules the world! O God, do you exist? You're there and You don't avenge it. How many more Russian crimes do You want—or—or are You a Russian too!!? My poor Father! The dear old man may be starving, my mother not able to buy bread? Perhaps my sisters have succumbed to the ferocity of Muscovite soldiery let loose? Oh Father, what a comfort for your old age! Mother! Poor suffering Mother, have you borne a daughter to see a Russian violate her very bones! Mockery! Has even her

'The Terror of the 29th,' the Warsaw Uprising.

[Emilia's] grave been respected? Trampled, thousands of other corpses are over the grave. What has happened to her [Konstancja]? Where is she? Poor girl, perhaps in some Russian's hands—a Russian strangling her, killing, murdering! Ah my Life, I'm here alone; come to me, I'll wipe away your tears, I'll heal the wounds of the present, remind you of the past—the days when there were no Russians, the days when the only Russians were a few who were very anxious to please you, and you were laughing at them because I was there. Have you your mother? Such a cruel mother, and mine is so kind. But perhaps I have no mother, perhaps some Russian has killed her, murdered. My sisters, raving, resist—father in despair, nothing he can do—and I here, useless! And I here with empty hands! Sometimes I can only groan, and suffer, and pour out my despair at the piano! God, shake the earth, let it swallow up the men of this age, let the heaviest chastisement fall on France, that would not come to help us—

—The bed I go to—perhaps corpses have lain on it, lain long—yet today that does not sicken me. Is a corpse any worse than I? A corpse knows nothing of father, of mother, of sisters, of Titus; a corpse has no beloved, its tongue can hold no conversation with those who surround it—a corpse is as colourless as I, as cold as I am cold to everything now—

—The clocks in the towers of Stuttgart strike the hours of the night. How many new corpses is this minute making in the world? Mothers losing children, children losing mothers. So much grief over the dead, and so much delight! A vile corpse and a decent one—virtues and vice are all one, they are sisters when they are corpses. Evidently, then, death is the best act of man. And what is the worst? Birth: it is direct opposition to the best thing. I am right to be angry that I came into the world. What use is my existence to anyone? I am not fit for human beings, for I have neither snout nor calves to my legs; and does a corpse have them? A corpse also has no calves, so it lacks nothing of a mathematical fraternity with death. Did she [Konstancja] love me, or was she only pretending? That's a knotty point to get over—Yes, no, yes, no, no, yes—finger by finger—Does she love me? Surely she loves me, let her do what she likes—

—Father! Mother! Where are you? Corpses? Perhaps some Russian has played tricks—oh wait—wait—But tears—they have not flowed for so long—oh, so long, so long I could not weep—how glad—how wretched—Glad and wretched—If I'm wretched, I can't be glad—and yet it is sweet—This is a strange state—but that is so with a corpse; it's well and not well with it at the same moment. It is transferred to a happier life and is glad, it regrets the life it is leaving and is sad. It must feel as I felt when I left off weeping. It was like some momentary death of feeling; for a moment I died in my heart; no, my heart died in me for a moment. Ah, why not for always! Perhaps it would be more endurable then. Alone! Alone! There are no words for my misery; how can I bear this feeling—

Possibly around this time Chopin contemplated or sketched the C minor saga closing his Op. 10 cycle. Common assumption has it that this most widely played of pieces, the so-called *Revolutionary* Study, was inspired by Warsaw's downfall. True or not – during the 19th century more than an occasional writer spun fanciful tales around Chopin's works – the rushing, torrent-like cascades of sound, the dramatic, rhetorical melody pausing for moments of lyrical repose before surging forth with

Panorama of Paris, woodcut 1852. High society and exiles. Hedonism and insurgency. Roses in the boudoir, cholera on the streets. A city in ferment. Refugees fleeing the Russians – the Great Emigration, from soldiers and poets to fallen nobility - guaranteed a strong Polish presence. The 'virtuous marketplace' and abuse-and-favour climate of France's jewel needed no reminding. It had a high prostitution rate with hundreds of registered *maisons de tolerance*, and an undeclared number of *grisettes* – 'young working women who are coquettish and flirtatious'. Artists' models, *danseuses* and actresses added to the temptations on offer - declined by Chopin, having already dallied elsewhere to personal cost ('the memory of Teressa [likely a *Wiener Dirne*] does not allow me to taste the forbidden fruit'). In 1831 Paris's population was estimated at around 786,000, many times greater than that of Warsaw.

renewed fury, inevitably invite extra-musical interpretation. 'Turbulent music' for future silent-film pianists and the 'photoplay music' age.

His immediate reaction passed, Chopin pulled himself together and set off on the last leg to Paris. He arrived in mid-September, on the 11th. In the French capital he found the environment he needed… the stage on which his finest hours were to be acted.

5. Paris I

'Paris is whatever you choose'

Chopin

For over forty years France had been the centre of turmoil and regeneration. Riding his Arabian charger into the modern age, Napoléon forged a new nation, occupied Europe, and won himself a podium in history. The defining triumph of his rule was the establishment of a modern administrative system, and the emergence of new liberties for the common majority, rights previously controlled by the nobility who'd cared little for the plight of the peasant population. On 14 July 1789, deprived of their freedom to express themselves, the people rose against the king, Louis XVI, and his queen, Marie Antoinette, storming the Bastille. Their grievances were well grounded. Put simply, how could a country be governed by a feeble king who sought only to satisfy his own pleasures – hunting, eating, mending clocks and sleeping in the council chamber of his lavish palace

Execution of Louis XVI (1754-93), 21 January 1793.

Marie Antoinette (1755-93),
guillotined 16 October 1793

at Versailles – and a queen who felt compelled in the national interest to retain just 500 servants and acquire only four new pairs of shoes a week?

The 1789 Revolution led to change, but extremists like Robespierre wanted to overthrow the monarchy altogether. Eventually they won the day. In 1793 Louis was guillotined and the First Republic declared. Out of chaos and the excesses of protest order finally emerged. New laws were introduced, the rights of the aristocracy withdrawn, the lot of the peasants improved, and slavery abolished.

The rise of Napoléon consecrated the First Republic. 'Roman'-style, he was elected Consul in 1799. The public voted, however, that he should be proclaimed Emperor, and in December 1804 he was duly crowned in Notre Dame, an action which earned critical condemnation (and Beethoven's famous rage). Originally a champion of *liberty*, he was now a dictator with absolute rule – from army orders to artistic comment. That said, his strong leadership *did* bring stability to an unbalanced France, as well as prosperity and security to a country which had long forgotten such virtues.

Dreams of conquest haunted Napoléon. They were ultimately his ruination. At the hands of Nelson, he faced naval defeat at Trafalgar in 1805 and his supremacy began to be questioned. The final test came in 1812 with the invasion of Russia. Count Philippe-Paul de Ségur, one of his generals and *aides-de-camp*, went on the campaign, later publishing an account of its hopes and hell*. In July 1812 he wrote: 'The Russian frontier stretched before us. Through the gloom our eager eyes strained to see into this glorious promised land. We imagined we heard the joyful shouts of the Lithuanians at the approach of their deliverers... We would be surrounded by love and gratitude.' In August Napoléon's men captured Smolensk on their way to Moscow: 'We passed through the smoking ruins in military formation, with our martial music and customary pomp, triumphant over this desolation, but with no other witness to our glory.' In September Moscow was reached, but Napoléon had miscalculated the onslaught of the Russian winter. Victory turned to defeat. Like hunted animals the Grand Army fled and collapsed slowly: 'This army had numbered one hundred thousand combatants on leaving Moscow. In twenty-five days it had been reduced to thirty-six thousand!... The silence was broken only by the crack of whips applied to horses... we dropped into hollows and had to climb back up the icy slopes, with men, horses and cannon rolling over each other in the darkness.'

This was the end. A last stand one Sunday at Waterloo in June 1815 resulted only in a morally and physically weakened *Armée du Nord* losing to the combined British and Prussian armies under Wellington and Blücher. With Napoléon's official abdication in 1814, the Congress of Vienna defined the limits of France and re-organised the structure of an occupied Europe. Louis XVIII, long recognised as the official king by the *émigré* French, came to the throne.

In the beginning Louis endeavoured to continue Napoléon's political reforms. But he was a weak man, contrasting his very different 'throwback' brother, Charles X. Charles, who succeeded him in 1824, was only interested in carrying on the tradition of pre-revolutionary France. A Bourbon, he'd spent an extravagant exile in Edinburgh and London, his wardrobe

* *Napoléon's Russian Campaign*, trans. J. David Townsend (London 1959) from *Histoire de Napoléon et de la Grande Armée pendant l'année 1812*.

Napoléon Bonaparte (1769-1821): Corsican general, First Consul, Emperor, reformer, 'world-spirit on horseback', prisoner in exile. 'My true glory is not to have won forty battles ... Waterloo will erase the memory of so many victories ... But what will live forever is my Civil Code'. After the 1838 portrait by Paul Delaroche, *Napoléon in his Study*, commissioned by the Dowager Countess of Sandwich and inspired by David's 1812 painting on the same subject.

including a different pair of jewelled shoe-buckles for each day of the year. He curbed civil liberties and chose formerly influential aristocrats as his advisers; he also imposed a press censorship and dismissed parliament. His interest in public affairs was minimal.

The spirit of '89 had been epoch-making, and the Russian defeat of Napoléon had spurred many countries to assert their identity if not their freedom. For how long now would the citizens of France remain silent? Progressive unrest reached a head in July 1830 when Paris became embroiled in another revolution: Charles X was overthrown and Louis-Philippe, Duke of Orleans, an opponent of the royalist régime and a supporter of democracy, was placed on the throne. The 'citizen king', Louis-Philippe was well-meaning but never really came to grips with the problems facing his people – leading in February 1848 to his abdication, the end of the so-called July Monarchy, and the *liberté, égalité, fraternité* flag of the Second Republic. Fleeing Paris in a cab, disguised as 'Mr. Smith', he spent his final days in England (in Claremont House near Esher, Surrey) as a guest of Queen Victoria.

The Paris intellectuals of the day were the defining Children of the Century, *les enfants du siècle*. Upholding freedom of speech and thought, their values were sharp and modern,

Above: Boulevard Poissonnière, Paris: painting by Isidore Dagnan, 1834.

Above right: Honoré de Balzac (1799–1850): etching by Pierre-Edmond-Alexandre Hédouin. 'One of the first among the greatest, one of the highest among the best' - Victor Hugo.

pared to the knuckle. They liked the idea of Danton's 'we need audacity, and yet more audacity, and always audacity!'. When, years later, Lamartine wrote of the 'brief, nervous, lucid style, stripped of phrases, robust of limb' associated with the old Savoyard Joseph-Marie de Maistre (1753–1821), in spirit neither 18th century 'soft' nor Gallic declamatory, he spoke for a movement as much as about an individual. 'Born and steeped in the breath of the Alps, it was virgin, it was young, it was harsh and savage; it had no human respect, it felt its solitude, it improvised depth and form all at once.'

* In 1838 he painted one of the most distinctive portraits of Chopin, highlighting the gaunt, haunted planes of the face that so typified the composer in his later years. See frontispiece, p.6.

Overnight Chopin found himself in the midst of some of the brightest minds ever to congregate in the same place at the same time. Victor Hugo, Balzac and Lamartine spearheaded the *literati*. Delacroix, of *Liberty leading the People* fame (commemorating the July Revolution), led the painters*. Among musicians easily the most radical were Alkan (Jewish, obsessive, pianistically titanic), Liszt (eighteen months younger than Chopin) and Berlioz, whose bold and brilliant *Symphonie fantastique: Épisode de la vie d'un Artiste* dedicated to the Tsar of Russia – dramatically breaking with Beethoven and the high classicists – had been premiered in Paris less than a year before Chopin's arrival.

Paris overwhelmed Chopin. But his letters show him taking life in his stride. Those displays of emotion and *angst* darkening the months before never quite go away – but become less outwardly apparent, reserved only for the most private confessions to the closest of intimates.

His first home – comfortable but expensive – was on the fifth floor of 27 Boulevard Poissonnière, a spacious, tree-lined avenue: 'A delightful lodging; I have a little room beautifully furnished with mahogany, and a balcony over the boulevard from which I can see from Montmartre to the Panthéon and the whole length of the fashionable quarter; many people envy my view, though not my stairs!' (18 November 1831).

His correspondence pictures the spirit of the city. 'Paris is whatever you choose,' he tells Titus. 'You can amuse yourself, be bored, laugh, cry, do anything you like, and nobody looks at

Friedrich Kalkbrenner (1785-1849). 'German codfish aristocrats [*Stockfiscke*] envy his elegant mien, his admirably attired form, his polish and sweetness, his whole candied sugar cake exterior, which is, however, disagreeably jarred to the calm observer by many "involuntary Berlinisms of the lowest class"' - Heinrich Heine.

and everyone goes his own way. I don't know where there can be so many pianists as in Paris…' Following custom, he had brought with him several letters of introduction from influential people in Vienna. One was to Ferdinando Paer, formerly conductor of the Court Theatre, who'd previously been associated with the Théâtre-Italien. As court musician to Napoléon he'd gone to Warsaw in 1806. Paer willingly introduced him to the most illustrious names, including Rossini, monarch of the opera house, Kalkbrenner, and the veteran, venerated Cherubini. Kalkbrenner made perhaps the greatest impression. A letter to Titus (12 December):

> You would not believe how curious I was about Herz, Liszt, Hiller and so on. They are all zero besides Kalkbrenner. I confess that I have played like Herz, but would wish to play like Kalkbrenner. If Paganini is perfection, Kalkbrenner is his equal but in quite another style. It is hard to describe to you his calm, his enchanting touch, his incomparable evenness, and the mastery that is displayed in every note; he is a giant walking over Herz and Czerny and all—and over me. What can I do about it? When I was introduced, he asked me to play something. I should have liked to hear him first, but knowing how Herz plays, I pocketed my pride and sat down. I played my E minor [Concerto], which the Rhinelanders… and all Bavaria have so raved about. I astonished Kalkbrenner, who at once asked me was I not a pupil of Field, because I have Cramer's method and Field's touch—that delighted me. I was still more pleased when Kalkbrenner, sitting down at the piano and wanting to do his best before me, made a mistake and had to break off! But you should have heard it when he started again: I had not dreamed of anything like it. Since then we meet daily; either he comes to me or I to him. On closer acquaintance, he has made me an offer: that I should study with him for three years and he will really make something out of me. I answered that I know how much I lack, but that I cannot exploit him, and three years is too much. But he has convinced me that I can play admirably when I am in the mood and badly when I am not, a thing which never happens to him.

Kalkbrenner's desire to teach Chopin met with strong family resistance. Elsner, too, was displeased. Everyone, especially

Nicholas, felt that although Chopin's only formal piano lessons had been in his formative youth under Żywny– he was, in effect, self-taught – he was brilliant enough and sufficiently highly regarded not to need a further *three* years of extra study.

Indecision troubled the young man. Where did his future lie – as a pianist or a composer? (That his playing and temperament were unsuited to the strenuous life of a virtuoso – he could never hope to emulate Liszt, for instance – only came to dawn on him later.) Elsner, following another agenda, insisted that he must devote himself to one pursuit – composition – arguing that Kalkbrenner's offer to teach him would only retard his development as a composer... and in any case what worth had a mere 'piano player'? He wanted Chopin to become a great nationalist opera composer, drawing on Poland's past for his inspiration. Yet while Chopin had a deep love for the stage, he knew well (and Elsner probably should have also) that he was singularly incapable of developing along such lines. (Elsner's vision would have to wait until Moniuszko in the 1840s.)

A letter to Elsner, 14 December 1831, puts his viewpoint, admitting further to his disillusionment as a composer, his lack of success, and his want of knowledge. If composers such as Meyerbeer (highly fashionable at the time) have difficulty in finding a platform for their music, what opportunity does *he* have? At least, he says, he still has some chance as a pianist – though not as a student of Kalkbrenner. 'Three years are a long time, too long; even Kalkbrenner now admits that.' The decision didn't disrupt their friendship: when the E minor Concerto was published in Paris in June 1833, the title page bore a dedication to 'Monsieur F[riedrich] Kalkbrenner'.

Chopin's efforts to become an established pianist, a player in the field, met with support from other budding musicians living in the metropolis, including Liszt and August Franchomme, a cellist who was to become a particularly close friend (after the piano, the cello was Chopin's favourite instrument: anticipating Brahms, 'cello' lines abound in his keyboard writing). Yet despite mixing with such ardent personalities, and his contact with the more revolutionary ideals of a progressive spirit like Berlioz, Chopin remained detached. His poetic insights and sensitive nuances, often experimental in effect, were of a different order of fervour and radicalism. The frequent political messaging of his peers didn't come naturally to him, not their ideaological trumpeting.

Louis-Philippe d'Orléans (1773-1850). 'What is there against him? That throne. Take away Louis-Philippe the king, there remains the man. And the man is good. He is good at times even to the point of being admirable' - Victor Hugo.

The purely fashionable, too, held no interest for him: honourable exceptions aside – Liszt principally – he never had any of the exhibitionist dross of the day on his piano. Bach and Mozart were, and would always be, his gods.

Paris during these months continued to suffer the fallout of the July Revolution. On Christmas Day (1831), Chopin writes to Titus:

> You know there is great distress here; the exchange is bad, and you can often meet ragged folk with important faces, and sometimes you can hear menacing remarks about the stupid Philippe [the king], who just hangs on by means of his ministers. The lower classes are thoroughly exasperated, and would be glad at any moment to change the character of their misery, but unfortunately the government has taken too many precautions in this matter: as soon as the smallest street crowds collect, they are dispersed by mounted *gendarmerie.*

He chronicles an 'enormous' demonstration, gathering momentum and size like a 'snowball', from eleven in the morning 'til eleven at night:

> Many were hurt... nevertheless a large crowd collected on the boulevards under my windows, joining those who arrived from the other side of the town. The police could do nothing with the surging mass; a detachment of infantry arrived; hussars, mounted *adjutants de place* [military police] on the pavements; the guard, equally zealous, shoving aside the excited and muttering crowd, seizing, arresting free citizens—nervousness, shops closing, groups of people at all the corners of the boulevards; whistles, galloping messengers, windows crammed with spectators (as at home on Easter Day)...
> I began to hope that perhaps something would get done, but it all ended with the singing of *Allons enfants de la patrie* [the *Marseillaise*] by a huge chorus at eleven at night. You will scarcely realise what an impression these menacing voices of an unsatisfied crowd produced on me.

6. Paris 2

'His character was not easy to grasp. It was composed of a thousand shades'

Franz Liszt

Chopin's first Paris concert, backed by Kalkbrenner among others, was billed for Christmas Day 1831, but one of the singers couldn't participate and it had to be postponed to January 15th. Then Kalkbrenner fell ill and it didn't finally take place until Saturday 25 February 1832*. The venue was the salon of Camille Pleyel, a man, contemporaries gossiped, 'as famous for his pianos as his wife's adventures'. The room, at 9 rue Cadet, was large with a vaulted ceiling, hung with chandeliers, and heavy velvet curtains draped behind the stage – an evocative backdrop to display Chopin's talents. He presented the E minor Concerto and *Là ci darem* Variations. No orchestra was available so he played the former with string quartet, the (reduced) accompaniment advantageously showcasing both himself and the music; and the latter as a solo. The evening was surely one of nostalgia. He was homesick, and the folk rhythms of the concerto's finale, coupled with the *maggiore* reverie of its nocturnal slow movement, must have generated bitter-sweet memories of childhood and Konstancja. He may even have heard of her marriage a few weeks earlier.

Chopin also took part in a performance of Kalkbrenner's recent *Grande Polonaise with Introduction and March* for six pianos, in which he was joined by, among others, George Onslow (a successful Anglo-Frenchmen from Clermont-Ferrand related paternally to the 1st Earl of Onslow) and Ferdinand Hiller. Hiller, a cultured, affable Jew from Frankfurt who later taught Max Bruch, had been a pupil of Hummel, and was to become a good friend of Chopin's. In 1829 he'd been the first pianist to play Beethoven's *Emperor* Concerto in Paris, conducted by Berlioz.

Chopin's reputation aroused so much interest that the concert was attended by many distinguished musicians and critics. Fétis, the most respected and feared commentator of the age, wrote that he found in 'M[onsieur] Chopin's inspirations

* Not the 26th as formerly supposed (Jean-Jacques Eigeldinger, *Revue de Musicologie* Vol. 94/ii, 2008).

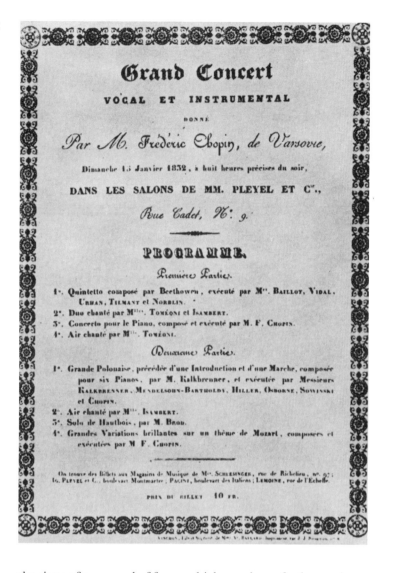

the signs of a renewal of forms which may henceforth exercise considerable influence upon this branch of the art' (*La revue musicale*, 3 March). Mendelssohn, wintering in the city, was also enthusiastic. One of Chopin's friends, Anton Orłowski, wrote home to Poland: 'Our dear Fritz has wiped the floor with all the pianists here: all Paris was stupefied'. Years later Liszt cameoed the moment: 'We remember his first appearance in the rooms of Pleyel, where we were so delighted that the most noisy applause seemed insufficient for the talent that was opening a new phase of poetic sentiment… he was not confused for a moment by the dazzlement or intoxication of the triumph. He accepted it without pride and without false modesty.'

The burgeoning relationship between Liszt and Chopin, so fabled in resonance, lasted less than ten years. It was to be a pretty one-sided affair. Liszt, the less refined of the two, was forward and ardent, Chopin discrete and reserved. One commentated, the other commented. Chopin respected Liszt's virtuosity, but, never living to see his post-1850 masterworks, thought he wasted too much time on worthless trifles: he knows 'everything better than anyone... he is an excellent binder who puts other people's work between his own covers... he is a clever craftsman without a vestige of talent'. Of Chopin's friendships with other arch-romantics of Liszt's disposition, it would probably be truer to say that his attachment to, say, Berlioz (whom he met at the end of 1832 and at whose house in Montmartre he was a frequent , if emotionally reserved, guest) was at a deeper level than anything experienced with Franz L.

The success of his début concert, and the hospitality of the city, so unlike Vienna, prompted Chopin to give another, and on 20 May he appeared at an important charity event in the concert hall of the Conservatoire, playing the first movement of the E minor. This time, however, the impression on the public was less favourable. The small tone Chopin produced from his piano failed to compete with the orchestra, and his scoring was criticised for a 'lack of lightness'. Again, it seemed, Chopin was faced with a setback, and he thought of going to England, even America – then enjoying a period of stability under their president, Andrew Jackson.

Fortuitously – with Paris in the grip of a cholera epidemic and funds at rock bottom – Prince Walenty Radziwiłł introduced him to the illustrious and immensely rich Baron Jacob Mayer de Rothschild, youngest son of the most important banking dynasty in 19th century Europe. Suddenly Chopin was welcomed by a family whose influence was far-reaching. Overnight he found himself in demand among the aristocracy. A decade later he recalled his gratitude by dedicating the Fourth Ballade to Baroness Charlotte, Jacob's first-born, who'd become his student in 1841.

Friendship with the Rothschilds saw Chopin's teaching diary expand rapidly: all the 'ladies of the Faubourg-Saint-Germain or of the Slavonic aristocracy exiled in Paris' flocked to his salon. Chopin's methods as a teacher were sound and beneficial. He insisted that all his pupils practise Clementi's *Gradus ad Parnassum*, and for gaining independence of fingers he found Bach's preludes and fugues from the *Forty Eight* 'indispensable'. More advanced pupils also learned his own works such as the studies. In playing scales he preferred to begin with that of B

The Hall of the Paris Conservatoire, March 1843: anonymous woodcut, *L'Illustration*.

major as this gave a good hand position; until this was perfected he would not teach other scales, and he regarded the white-key one of C major as the most difficult to execute properly. He considered three hours practice sufficient if a student was not to get tired or bored with the music, and he always looked for a pure, unforced tone, and a perfect *legato* touch when required. Interpretatively, he disliked the unnecessary exaggeration and forced dramatic effects admired by his contemporaries. His choice of fingering was often unorthodox if this helped gain greater fluency and *cantabile*, and he was among the earliest teachers to recognise the importance of a psychological approach towards his pupils, habitually taking individual needs and differences into account.

For his lessons, usually five a day, he received a fee of 20 francs* each, left on the mantelpiece (adding up to around £300 daily in modern terms); but charged more when teaching privately in pupils' homes. His example and pedagogy influenced many. Yet, paradoxically, he left almost no one to carry on his tradition (unlike, Liszt or Henselt whose students

* In a letter from London, 17 July 1848, Chopin says that 'one pound and fifteen shilling… comes to 45 francs', yielding a rule-of-thumb exchange rate of 25.7 francs to the pound.

defined epochs and schools). Less than a dozen made the profession.

Increasingly better off, Chopin moved into a comfortably appointed second floor apartment in July 1832 – 4 rue Cité Bergère.

> I am in the highest society: I sit with ambassadors, princes, ministers and even don't know now how it came about, because I did not try for it... Though this is my first year among the artists here [mid-January 1833], I have their friendship and respect. One proof of respect is that even people with huge reputations [for example, Pixis and Kalkbrenner] dedicate their compositions to me before I do so to them... finished artists take lessons from me and couple my name with Field's. In short, if I was not stupider than I am, I should think myself at the apex of my career, yet I know how much I still lack to reach perfection.

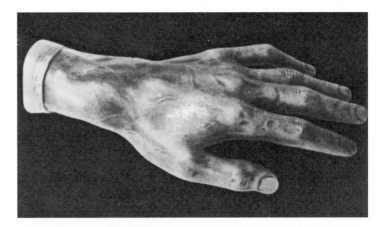

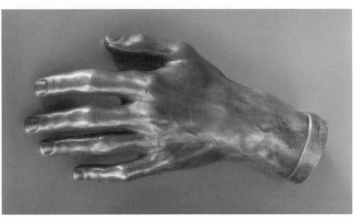

Chopin's left hand modelled by Auguste Clésinger, 17 October 1849. 'Unlike Clementi, Hummel, Kalkbrenner or Czerny, Chopin did not create a school or institute a set tradition. It was not in his nature to impose his personality on pupils, in the way that the Liszt of Weimar did. Too much of an aristocrat and poet to become a leader, Chopin was content to suggest and imply, winning devotion without any attempt to convince' - Jean-Jacques Eigeldinger.

He was able to afford his own man-servant* and a carriage, while his clothes and white gloves came from the most fashionable Paris shops: 'without them I should not have *bon ton*'.

Publishers, French and foreign, heeded his growing popularity. In early 1833 he had the satisfaction of seeing the publication of the Nocturnes, Op. 9 (No. 2 enjoying particular success because it wasn't excessively difficult), two sets of Mazurkas, and the early Op. 8 Piano Trio completed in Warsaw. Compositions in hand included the first six of his second set of Studies, Op. 25, finalised in Dresden in 1836, and the first movement of a new piano concerto – which finally became the rarely heard solo *Allegro de Concert*, Op. 46, finished in 1841.

On Christmas Day 1832 John Field premiered his Seventh Concerto at the Paris Conservatoire (having much earlier – in February – appeared at a Philharmonic Society concert in London). Field, Chopin's model in the opinion of many, had once been 'the archtype of the "artistic" concert soloist, who by casting a spell could shrink the walls of a great auditorium, and create in the fancy of the audience a dialogue between his soul and each listener's' (Nicholas Temperley). By 1832, in ill health, he was in the twilight of his years. Rapier-fingered Liszt admired the fluency of playing but found it 'sleepy' and 'lacking in vitality': 'does he bite?' A friend reported Chopin saying that he had 'no speed, no elegance... incapable of executing difficulties: in a word, feeble'.

On 2 April 1833, at a benefit concert in the Salle Favart for Berlioz's future wife, the Anglo-Irish actress Harriet Smithson, Chopin appeared with Liszt, playing Onslow's Duet Sonata in F minor. On 20 June he wrote to Hiller, 'without knowing what

Liszt's left hand: plaster cast. 'Flexing and relaxing the fingers in all directions ... for hours on end, while at the same time reading to avoid boredom' - Auguste Boissier on Liszt's daily regime, Paris 1832.

* 'A man-servant is an article of luxury in Paris, and very rarely to be found in the home of an artist!' (Wilhelm von Lenz, 1842).

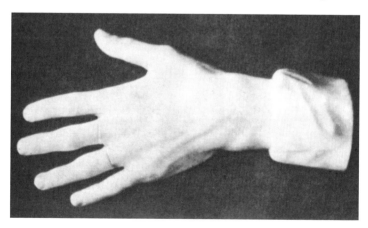

my pen is scribbling because at this moment Liszt is playing my *études* and transporting me outside my respectable thoughts. I should like to steal from him the way to play my own *études*.' The Op. 10 set had just been published by Maurice Schlesinger, inscribed to Liszt, 'son ami' (the later London engraving adding Hiller as joint-dedicatee). The E minor Concerto was issued at the same time.

In December a second set of Nocturnes (Op. 15) was published, dedicated to Hiller, and on the 15th of the month Chopin joined Liszt and Hiller at the Conservatoire for a performance of Bach's D minor Concerto for three pianos.

Notwithstanding a growing friendship with Bellini – the poet-prince of *bel canto* – 1834 was a fairly uneventful year. There were no important concerts until December, and Chopin's only excursion away was with Hiller to attend the Lower Rhineland Music Festival, held in Aachen in May. Here he renewed his friendship with Mendelssohn, who wrote to his mother (23 May):

Corrected German title page of Chopin's Twelve Studies, Op. 10. The original French, German and English editions identified Liszt as 'J.' rather than 'F.' 'Those who have distorted fingers may put them right by practising these studies; but those who have not, should not play them, at least not without having a surgeon at hand' - Heinrich Rellstab.

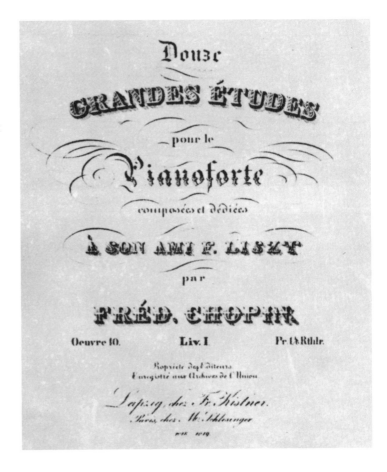

Felix Mendelssohn (1809-47): after a painting by Carl Jäger, 1870. 'People often complain that music is so ambiguous ... whereas everyone understands words; with me it is exactly the reverse ... [words] seem so ambiguous, so vague, so unintelligible when compared with genuine music, which fills the soul with a thousand things better than words'.

... when I was coming up [after a rehearsal of Handel's oratorio, *Deborah*] who should stumble right into my arms but Ferdinand Hiller, who almost hugged me to death with joy. He had come from Paris to hear the oratorio, and Chopin had left his scholars in the lurch, and had come with him, and thus we met again. I had now my full share of delight in the Musical Festival, for we three lived together, and got a private box in the theatre (where the oratorio is performed), and of course next morning we betook ourselves to the piano, where I had the greatest enjoyment. They have both improved much in execution, and, as a pianist, Chopin is now one of the very first of all. He produces new effects [pedalling, for example], like Paganini

Adam Mickiewicz (1798-1855): after a portrait by Louis Croutelle, 1828. '... he looked down and measured the strings with his eye; he joined his hands and smote with the two hammers in unison: the blow was so artistic, so powerful, that the strings rang like brazen trumpets, and from the trumpets a well-known song floated to the heavens, a triumphal march, Poland has not yet perished ...' - *Pan Tadeusz*, Book XII.

on his violin, and accomplishes wonderful passages, such as no one could formerly have thought practical. Hiller, too, is an admirable player—vigorous and yet playful. Both, however, rather toil in the Parisian spasmodic and impassioned style, too often losing sight of time and sobriety and of true music; I, again, do so perhaps too little—thus we all three mutually learn something and improve each other, while I feel rather like a schoolmaster, and they a little like *mirliflores* or *incroyables* [French dandies]. After the festival we travelled together to Düsseldorf, and passed a most agreeable day there, playing and discussing music; then I accompanied them yesterday to Cologne. Early this morning they went off to Coblenz *per* steam—I in the other direction—and the pleasant episode was over!

Among Chopin's works published in 1834 were the *Fantasia on Polish Airs*, the *Krakoviak* and the *Grande valse brillante*,

The Chopin family apartment, Warsaw 1832. Left wing of Krasiński Palace, second floor, destroyed in World War II. Pen sketch by Antoni Kolberg, lost in 1942.

Op. 18 (autograph dated 10 July 1833*). He also completed various of his Op. 25 Studies, including the well known *Butterfly* (No. 9) and the *Allegro con fuoco* in B minor (No. 10) – Hans von Bülow's 'Asiatic wilderness' renowned for its double-octave passages, the first time Chopin had penned such a muscular torrent of heavy artillery 'Lisztian' octaves.

For Chopin and his cohorts of the Polish Literary Society – all keen students of Polish literature, otherwise hardly known in purely French circles – 1834 was emotionally towering for the publication in June, in Paris, of Adam Mickiewicz's national epic *Pan Tadeusz*. Victor Hugo believed that 'to speak of Mickiewicz is to speak of the beautiful, the just, the true; is to speak of the cause whose soldier he was, of the duty whose hero he was, of the liberty whose apostle he was, of the deliverance whose forerunner he was'. In *Pan Tadeusz,* Mickiewicz painted an intense picture of Poland, its traditions, symbols and spirit, past and present. The rallying cry of an era.

* One of the first pieces to be finished in his new flat at 5 Chaussée d'Antin - a luxurious place he shared first with a heavy-smoking physician from Warsaw, Aleksander Hofman; and then, from April 1834, with Jan Matuszyński, in Paris to study medicine.

7. Interlude

'In vain did I give a ring'

Stefan Witwicki

Maria Wodzińska (1819-96): pencil self-sketch, 1836.

* Compromisingly, the story goes, Liszt had used Chopin's rue de Montblanc quarters for a liaison with Marie Pleyel, the much younger wife of Camille – whom she'd married in 1832 on the rebound from Berlioz.

In April 1835 Chopin gave his last two public concerts in Paris. Their relative failure decided him against furthering a career as a concert pianist. His confiding approach to the instrument was at variance with the young *Klaviertigeren* of the day, and he found the element of competition uncomfortable. Besides, his success as a teacher and composer was blossoming – and composition was where his real heart lay.

At the first concert, a charity event for Polish orphans at the Théâtre-Italien on the 4th, playing an Érard, he offered the E minor Concerto and, despite a recent distasteful falling-out *, duetted with Liszt. At the second, on the 26th, he gave the first performance of the *Andante spianato* and *Grande Polonaise* for piano and orchestra in the box-lined auditorium of the Conservatoire – in the context of a largely Beethoven programme conducted by François Habeneck, then 'entrenched in the most powerful executive position in the Paris musical world' (David Cairns). Following this he occasionally played to private gatherings but made no attempt again to seek engagements professionally. 'Liszt, in 1835, represented *a merveilleux* the prototype of the virtuoso; while in my opinion Chopin personified the poet. The first aimed at effect and posed as the Paganini of the piano; Chopin, on the other hand, seemed never to concern himself about the public, and to listen only to the inner voices. He was unequal; but when inspiration took hold of him he made the keyboard sing in an ineffable manner' (Gustave Chouquet).

To this period belongs the the well-known Fantaisie Impromptu (published posthumously in 1855), together with various *brillante* concert waltzes, some mazurkas, and the first official set of Polonaises (Op. 26) – two dramatic pieces in minor keys. In February 1835 the First Scherzo was published by Schlesinger, and in August his English publishers, Wessel & Stodart of 1 Soho Square, brought out their own edition. The owner of the firm, Christian Rudolph Wessel, came originally from Bremen in Germany, and had started the company in 1825.

An astute businessman, he saw the potential in Chopin's work but wasn't generous with his money (just £15 for the Op 28 *Préludes*, around £1,200 in modern currency); his whimsical provision of fanciful titles enraged the composer.

During August Chopin met his parents for the first time since leaving Warsaw. They were in Karlovy Vary (Karlsbad) for a month's holiday, and Chopin wrote to Ludwika in Poland: 'I can't collect my thoughts or write anything but our happiness at being together at this moment. To think that what I had so long only dared hope for has today come true, and happiness, happiness, happiness is here!'

Karlovy Vary was a beautiful spa, situated along the banks of the Ohre river: to the north rose the peaks of the Ore Mountains, while some way to the south the great expanse of the Bohemian Forest stretched to the Danube. For a moment Chopin forgot his troubles, the magic of his childhood flooded back, he found himself in a state of cosseted bliss. Once Nicholas and Justyna returned to Warsaw – Monday 14 September – he would not see them again.

Days later Chopin renewed his friendship with the Wodziński family. Living in Geneva, they'd left Poland during the 1831 revolt, and in 1835 were visiting Dresden for the summer. As a child Chopin had spent happy hours with the boys of the family who lived in the Chopin household when they were pupils at the Lyceum. The Wodzińskis had a daughter, Maria. Since his *frisson d'amour* with Konstancja, Chopin had been wary in his emotional dalliances – but he found a chord of sympathy in Maria and fell for her looks and charms. She was a good pianist – good enough to later play one of Chopin's ballades at a public concert in Warsaw – and on the 24th he wrote for her the A flat waltz Op. 69 No. 1 she later called *l'Adieu*. Maria's mother, prone to think of Chopin as her 'fourth son', realised his feelings and didn't discourage them. Others noticed, too, one old friend writing to Ludwika: 'Oh, we know Maria has won his heart…'

On 26 September Chopin left Dresden for Leipzig. At the home of the teacher and critic Friedrich Wieck, least pleasant of men, he met Mendelssohn and, for the first time, Schumann. Also present was Wieck's daughter, Clara, just turned sixteen. She admired Chopin's manners, music, and style of playing and as early as July 1832, aged twelve, had performed the *Là ci darem* Variations at a Musikalische Akademien in Leipzig *. Chopin declared her to be 'the only woman in Germany who

Clara Schumann *née* Wieck (1819-96). 'There is nothing that surpasses the joy of creation, if only because through it one wins hours of self-forgetfulness, when one lives in a world of sound'.

* An entry in her diary from the previous year, 8 June 1831, noted: 'Chopin's Variations Op. 2, which I learned in eight days, is the hardest piece I have seen or played till now. This original and inspired composition is still so little known that almost all pianists and teachers consider it incomprehensible and impossible to play'.

can play my music'.

Mendelssohn left an account of the visit in a letter to his sister, Fanny, 6 October:

> I cannot deny, dear Fanny, that I have lately found you by no means do [Chopin] justice in your judgement of his talents; perhaps he was not in a humour for playing when you heard him, which may not infrequently be the case with him. But his playing has enchanted me afresh, and I am persuaded that if you, and my father also, had heard some of his better pieces, as he played them to me, you would say the same. There is something thoroughly original in his pianoforte playing, and at the same time so masterly, that he may be called a most perfect virtuoso; and as in music I like and rejoice in every style of perfection, that day was most agreeable to me… It was so pleasant for me to be once more with a thorough musician, and not with those half virtuosos and half classics, who would gladly combine in music *les honneurs de la vertu et les plaisirs du vice*, but with one who has his perfect and well-defined phrase; and however far asunder we may be in our different spheres, still I can get on famously with such a person, but not with those half-and-half people.

Chopin: watercolour by Maria Wodzińska, Mariánské Lázně [Marienbad] August 1836.

Sunday evening was really very remarkable, when Chopin made me play over my oratorio [*St. Paul*] to him, while curious Leipzigers stole into the room to see him, and when between the first and second part he dashed into his new *études* and a new concerto [possibly the *Allegro de Concert* but more likely the E minor Concerto], to the amazement of the Leipzigers, and then I resumed my *St. Paul*—it was just as if a Cherokee and a Kaffir had met to converse. He has also such a lovely new *notturno* [Op. 27 No. 2], a considerable part of which I learnt by ear… So we got on most pleasantly together, and he promised faithfully to return in the course of the winter, if I would undertake to compose a new symphony and to perform it in his honour.

For Chopin, however, the winter was to pass in Paris. Despite endeavouring to hide the fact, he was once again seriously ill (the previous March he'd been coughing up blood). With no one hearing from him, rumour spread that he was dead. This sort of talk was the last thing he wanted the Wodzińskis to hear. How could they possibly let their daughter marry a weakling at death's door? Maria seems to have shrugged it off, but her mother monitored the situation warily.

In July 1836 the Wodzińskis invited Chopin to stay with them at Mariánské Lázně (Marienbad), another Bohemian spa near Karlovy Vary, noted for its precisely laid out grounds and surrounding hills. Chopin accepted, and August was spent with Maria. They made music and had long country walks: for Chopin it was a time of happiness. When the Wodzińskis left for Dresden in early September, Chopin followed. Here he composed the dreamily flowing Study in A flat which opens Op. 25, and also a song called *Pierścień* (The Ring). This was to words by Witwicki and its sentiments – like those of the same poet's *Smutna rzeka* set by Chopin some years earlier – seem to voice particularly personal feelings and thoughts:

… and I already loved you,
and for your left little finger
a silver ring I gave you.

Others have married girls
I faithfully loved;
there came a young lad, a stranger,
though I gave a ring.

Robert Schumann (1810-56): after a painting by Carl Jäger, 1871. 'I am drawn to compose! And yet, I would not like to tear myself-away from my Chopin'.

Robert Schumann

Musicians were invited
at the wedding I sang!
To another you became a wife,
I still loved.

Today the girls jeered at me,
bitterly I wept:
in vain have I been faithful and constant,
in vain did I give a ring.*

The following day, Friday the 9th, at the 'grey hour' (twilight) Chopin proposed. Maria accepted, but her family intervened, placing him on probation for of good behaviour. In particular he had to avoid late nights in the salons of Paris. 'Keep well, everything depends on that.'

Chopin left on the 11th, and passing through Leipzig spent time the following lunchtime with Schumann, playing parts of his, as yet, unfinished Second Ballade as well as the first two *études* from Op. 25. In his diary Schumann opined of the former that it

* Translated Bernard Jacobson.

Second Ballade, autograph ending. The inscription at the end is in another hand. 'Music does not exist in a single, correct version. It constantly changes over time. Chopin reminds us of that because he himself kept changing his music. Whenever we perform or listen to it, our experience is different from the last' – John Rink.

* Two years later Schumann dedicated his *Kreisleriana* to Chopin, who returned the compliment on publication of the Second Ballade.

was 'dearer to me than anything'*; the latter he pictured in the *Neue Zeitschrift für Musik*, 22 December 1837:

> Let one imagine that an Aeolian harp had all the scales and that an artist's hand had mingled them together in all kinds of fantastic decorations, but in such a way that you could always hear a deeper fundamental tone and a softly singing melody—there you have something of a picture of his playing. It is wrong to suppose that he brought out distinctly every one of the little notes: it was rather a billowing of the chord of A flat, swelled here and there by the [right] pedal… When the study was ended you feel as you do after a blissful vision, seen in a dream, which, already half-awake, you would fain recall… and then he played the second, in F minor… so charming, dreamy and soft, just as if a child were singing in its sleep.

Ever since reviewing the *Là ci darem* Variations, Schumann had held Chopin the highest regard, in 1834-35 penning a delicate musical portrait in *Carnaval*, and in 1835-36 drafting a set of variations on the G minor Nocturne from Op. 15 – 'the most terrifying declaration of war against a whole musical past'. His fantasy, the schizophrenia of his art, his way of thinking, wasn't to everyone's liking. Chopin – the aesthete sharing his confidences with few, embarrassed by attention: 'he listens reluctantly when one speaks of his works,' Schumann observed – found it hard to reciprocate and may even have been irritated by the effusiveness dispensed. When the German edition of the Second Ballade appeared in Leipzig in October 1840, the dedication was politely formal: '*Monsieur* Robert Schumann' – a dimension away from the '*son ami* [F.] Liszt' of the Op. 10 Studies, or the '*Seinem Freunde* Herrn F. Chopin' of *Kreisleriana*.

In Paris come the end of September Chopin was back to his socialising lifestyle, having taken a new 'exceptionally nice' apartment at 38 Chaussée d'Antin, complete with Polish servant. But as winter gripped so his health deteriorated, influenza, ostensibly, confining him to bed. The Wodziński family made up their minds: Maria could not marry him. She had no say in the matter. On the road to recovery, Chopin wrote letters and sent presents but the gestures fell on barren ground. No one replied. When they did eventually, the tone was unmistakeable: so far as all were concerned he had failed his 'probation'. 'Adieu. Do not forget us' were Maria's last words. Resigned, he bundled together his letters and Maria memories with a pink ribbon, writing on them simply 'Moja bieda', 'My Misery' (August 1837?). They remained with him for the rest of his life.

For a while mood and music seemed to go hand-in-hand: witness the Second Scherzo with its contrasts of storm and calm; or the ('F'/'M'-ciphered) Funeral March in B flat minor

'My Misery'.

– sketched by Chopin in September 1837, the break-up with Maria still fresh – incorporated later in the Second Sonata. Intimate introspection darkens too a contribution to a variation cycle, *Hexameron*, stitched together by Liszt on 'Suoni la tromba e intrepido', the Act II *marcia* from Bellini's last opera, *I Puritani* (produced at the *Théâtre-Italien*, 24 January 1835). Commissioned by Princess Cristina Trivulzio di Belgioioso, once the wealthiest heiress in Italy, a 'bird of curious plumage' and extraordinary life, *Hexameron* 'had no pretension or intention of doing anything but entertaining a crowd of rich patricians who were to be relieved of a considerable sum of money for a worthy cause [Italian refugees]': 'an omnibus of musical styles,

Hexameron, title page of 1st Austrian edition: Tobias Haslinger, Vienna February 1839.

Liszt caricatured by George Sand:
pen-and-ink, September 1836.

Paris 1837, a microcosm of some aspects of Liszt and one of the most interesting historical documents from the wild and woolly days when pianists were composers and composers were pianists' (Raymond Lewenthal). Liszt's involvement was extensive but the individual numbers still retained plenty of character and identity: Chopin's 17-bar murmur besides, there were inclusions from Czerny and Thalberg as well as Herz and Pixis, two especially fancied *salon* spinners of the hour.

During these months Chopin acquired a new friend in the seventeen-year-old Charles Hallé. Of German extraction, Hallé, subsequently first Principal of the Royal Manchester College of Music, lived in Paris between 1836 and 1848. His letters home make evocative reading, particularly in their references to Chopin:

> I went to dine with Baron Eichthal, where I was very cordially treated, and where I heard—*Chopin*. That was beyond all words. The few senses I had have quite left me. I could have jumped into the Seine. Everything I hear now seems so insignificant, that I would rather not hear it at all. Chopin! He is no man, he is an angel, a god (or what can I say more?). Chopin's compositions played

Charles Hallé (1819-95). Born Karl Halle in Hagen, Westphalia, Hallé changed his name on moving to England in 1848. 'Chopin carried you with him into a dreamland, in which you would have lived for ever'

by Chopin! That is a joy never to be surpassed... Kalkbrenner compared to Chopin is a child. I say this with the completest conviction. During Chopin's playing I could think of nothing but elves and fairy dances, such a wonderful impression do his compositions make. There is nothing to remind one that it is a human being who produces this music. It seems to descend from heaven—so pure, and clear, and spiritual. I feel a thrill each time I think of it. If Liszt plays *still better*, then the devil take me if I don't shoot myself on the spot [2 December 1836].

Later, in his *Autobiography*, he leaves a pen-sketch of Chopin the man:

With greater familiarity my admiration increased, for I learned to appreciate what before had principally dazzled me. In personal appearance he was also most striking, his clear-cut features, diaphanous complexion, beautiful brown waving hair, the fragility of his frame, his aristocratic bearing, and his princelike manners, singling him out, and

making one feel the presence of a superior man *. Meeting
often, we came into closer contact, and although at that
time I never exhibited what small powers I might possess
as a pianist, he knew me as an ardent student, and divined
that I not merely admired but understood him. With time
our acquaintance developed into real friendship, which I
am happy to say remained undisturbed until the end of his
too short life.

The winter and spring behind, relying on a smattering of
English picked up from lessons with a drunk Irishman in 1829,
Chopin made a fleeting fortnight's visit across the Channel in
July 1837, a few weeks after the young Victoria had been crowned
queen. Staying at the exclusive Sablonnière Hotel on the corner
of Cranbourn Street and Leicester Square (the former site of
Hogarth's house), he and Pleyel went to Windsor. Punts frequented
the Thames and open carriages were seen in the Great Park. The
sights were 'done' and both Chopin and Pleyel were depressed yet
fascinated by the dank chambers of the Tower. They also visited
Blackwall (famous for its fish dinners) and Richmond. 'The English
women, the horses, the palaces, the carriages, the wealth, the
splendour, the space, the trees – everything from soap to razors –
it's all extraordinary, all uniform, all very proper, all well-washed
BUT as black as a gentleman's bottom!' (writing to his friend and
associate Julian Fontana). Chopin didn't want his presence known
– though he did consent to play once at 46 Bryanston Square,
Marylebone, home of James Shudi Broadwood, High Sheriff of
Surrey and eldest son of the English piano manufacturer John
Broadwood.

Inscribed to Marie d'Agoult née de Flavigny, 'countess of
the golden hair', then living with Liszt, the second volume of
Studies, Op. 25, was published in October. The Liszt-d'Agoult
affair had for some time been a talking point of Parisian society,
and, though becoming sour and troubled, it continued to provide
a public wanting salacious gossip with as much diversion as the
latest adventures of Madame Pleyel, Marie Duplessis 'la dame
aux camélias' (loved by Liszt and Dumas), or La Païva (Herz's
mistress), the most illustrious French grande horizontale of the 19th
century. Disinclined to dabble, rebound or not, Chopin noted this
world and its tensions, its duels and jealousies, from the sidelines. It
needed the most exotic woman of a generation to walk into his life
to plunge him into the middle of it, endowing history with one of
the great , not to say baffling, liaisons of the Romantic age.

* Chopin's 1837 French passport
to London details the following
physical characteristics: 'height -
1 metre 70 cm [5'7"]; hair,
eyebrows and facial growth –
blond forehead, nose, mouth
– normal; eyes – blue-grey; face
oval; complexion fair'. His weight
the following year was a slight
seven stones (99 pounds, 45 kilos).

8. George Sand

'Chopin had little strength, but nobody could approach him in grace and elegance, and when he embellished, it was always the apotheosis of good taste… The Raphael of the piano, though one must not seek his Madonnas in churches – but in Life'

Wilhelm von Lenz

'A thinking bosom', 'descendant of a Polish king and a Paris bird seller', Amantine Aurore Lucile Dupin, Baronne Dudevant – the novelist George Sand (1804-76) – was Chopin's fourth romance. Neither contemporary (de Moriolles, Gładkowska) nor younger (Wodzińska) but older (by nearly six years), a Cancerian to his Pisces, as volatile and free in the art of love as he was abstaining and shy, so different 'from those fair-haired, those angelic, Polish ladies for whom, till then, he had entertained so chaste a passion!' (André Maurois), Sand married at eighteen. Casimir her husband, Dudevant of the long nose, was a 'thoroughly nice' but dull, unimaginative fellow who cared little for his strong-willed bride. For a time she reconciled herself to the situation and in their 'gentleman's residence' at Nohant (in the Berry region of France, 185 miles south of Paris, where she had been brought up as a child) made every effort to please him. She even stopped playing music – 'because the sound of the piano drove you away'. Casimir, it appears, remained unmoved and the marriage disintegrated into a contract of convenience. After nine years Sand had had enough, and in early 1831 came to Paris, writing for *Figaro* and, from 1832, *Revue des Deux Mondes*. Here she could mix freely with musicians, writers, painters and political movers. There were no inhibitions: their enthusiasm for life was hers to share. An independent, forthright streak began to emerge. To her mother she wrote: 'What I want is not society, noise, theatres, clothes… it's liberty. Here [in Paris] I can go out when I like, at ten o'clock or midnight, that's my business.'

From *hookah* and *havana* to trousers and high-boots, stove-hat and collar, Sand was her own woman. Not everyone warmed to her. To Baudelaire she was a 'stupid, heavy and garrulous slut'. To others a 'man-eating transvestite lesbian

Delacroix's *George Sand Dressed as a Man*, November 1834, following her break-up with Alfred de Musset. 'Significant as the first visualisation of the new female power Sand had achieved through her literary transvestism and easy manipulation of cultural codes of behaviour' - Janis Bergman-Carton.

Victor Hugo (1802-85). 'Music expresses that which cannot be put into words and that which cannot remain silent'.

nymphomaniac', gutter-tongued as a lighterman. To the Victorians a home-wrecker without moral scruples. To the oppressed and abused a defender of rights, a feisty left-wing 'socialist' with 'a powerful instinct for protest'. Liszt, Delacroix, Flaubert, Balzac, Gautier, de Musset... minds thespian and political... aristocrats, revolutionaries and dreamers... perfumed exquisites... circumscribed the religiously liberated, lotus-land world to which she was queen. Womanhood, gender and moral equaliy, mattered to her. 'Men insufficiently understand that their pleasure is our martyrdom' (February 1843). 'No man should obey a woman – that would be monstrous; no man should give orders to a woman – that is despicable' (April 1848). During the culminant years of her life she witnessed radical, momentous things. Friedrich Engels's *The Condition of the Working Class in England* appeared in 1845; three years later he wrote the *Communist Manifesto* with Karl Marx, ending with the celebrated call-to-arms 'Let the ruling classes tremble at a Communistic revolution. The proletariat have nothing to lose but their chains. They have a world to win... Working Men of All Countries, Unite!'. In 1867 Marx published the first volume of *Das Kapital*, laying the political foundation of the labour movement. Trade unionism was legalised in Britain in 1871.

Sand's arrival in Paris, a few months before Chopin, marked the start of her career as a novelist and playwright. Her literary talent may have been overshadowed by contemporaries like Hugo, Balzac, Lamartine and Stendahl, but her work even so enjoyed wide popularity, with subjects ranging from the sentimental *Indiana* *, through the social observation of *Lélia*, to simple rusticity – *François le Champi*. All in all she wrote around eighty books, some of an autobiographical nature. Many were dramatised.

A single mother in her thirties with fledgling children – Maurice (1823–89) and Solange (1828–99) – enjoying her latest *amour*, the dramatist Félicien Mallefille, Sand was close to Liszt and Marie d'Agoult. Towards the end of October 1836 she attended one of the Countess's *soirées* at the Hôtel de France where the musical and literary celebrities of the day gathered regularly. Chopin went, too. This was their first meeting. Just engaged to Maria, he was repulsed – 'what an unpleasant woman, that Mrs Sand! Is she really a woman? I allow myself to doubt'. Yet a week later, 5 November, we see her, Liszt and d'Agoult in Chopin's rooms at 38 Chaussée d'Antin; and on

13 December she attends a *soirée* he is giving. One of the guests, Jósef Brzowski, described the occasion:

> Madame G. Sand, dark, dignified and cold… Her dress fantastic (obviously proclaiming her desire to be noticed), composed of a white frock with a crimson sash and a kind of white shepherdess's corsage with crimson buttons. Her dark hair parted in the middle, falling in curls on both sides of her face and secured with a ribbon around her brow. Nonchalantly she took her place on the sofa near the fireplace, and, lightly blowing out clouds of smoke from her cigar, answered briefly but seriously the questions of the men sitting beside her… After Liszt and he had played a sonata, Chopin offered his guests ices. George Sand, wedded to her sofa, never quit her cigar for a moment.

Chopin held back. When Sand – now legally separated from her husband – invited him to spend the spring of 1837 at her country estate, with Liszt and Marie d'Agoult – 'I idolize him' – he declined. Maria may have been lost to him. But he still hoped. Sand waited.

Early the following year, 1838, Chopin appeared at the court

Above: Marie d'Agoult (1805-76) by Henri Lehmann, 1843. Her literary work appeared under the male pseudonym 'Daniel Stern'.

Below: Chopin: pencil drawing by Jakob Goetzenberger, October 1838.

of Louis-Philippe in the Tuileries, and at Rouen (reviving the E minor Concerto). 'To the question as to who is the foremost pianist in the world, Liszt or Thalberg, there is only one answer: Chopin' (*Revue et Gazette Musicale de Paris*, 25 March). At the showrooms of the piano-maker Jean-Henri Pape (3 March), he joined Alkan, Adolf Gutmann and Pierre Zimmermann (powerhouse pianists all), tackling Beethoven's Seventh Symphony arranged for eight hands, an event (the score is lost) he declined to repeat.

By the end of April, Sand, 'poetic cigars'* from the Orient rarely far away, was back on the scene. She and Chopin share trysts in a 'maiden room' she'd rented in rue Lafitte. 'We adore you.' And *soirée* away the evenings with Delacroix, Victor Hugo, Countess Carlotta Marliani (French-born wife of the Spanish Consul) and the actress Marie Dorval, Fryderyk playing late into the night. 'Darling,' she writes to Carlotta in Paris, 23 May 1838… 'in love-time the weather is changeable. There's a lot of YES and NO with ifs and buts in the course of a week, and one will often say in the morning, "This is unbearable," only to say in the evening, "This is absolute heaven"…' At the end of May, however, Count Wojciech Grzymała – mutual older friend and confidante, financially wily and amorously adventurous, a veteran of Borodino – wrote an unexpected letter (at Chopin's behest?) warning her off. From Nohant, pouring out her every thought, she dispatched a 32-page, 5,000-word reply/ultimatum, typically in style and (dense) manner:

> It would never occur to me to doubt the sincerity of your advice, my dear friend… give me a clear, straightforward and categorical answer. This young lady [Maria – whom Grzymała must have led her to believe was still in the picture] whom he wants or ought, or thinks he ought, to love, is she the right one to secure his happiness or is she likely to deepen his sufferings and melancholy? I am not asking whether he loves her or whether she returns his love, or whether he loves her more than me. I have a pretty good notion, judging by my own feelings, of what must be going on inside him. What I want to know is which of the *two of us* he must forget or give up, if he is to have any peace or happiness or indeed any life at all, for his nature seems too unstable and too frail to be able to stand up to great anguish. I don't want to play the part of the evil spirit… I will not battle with his childhood

* Opium, maybe hashish.

friend if she is a pure and lovely Alice [*une belle et pure Alice*]; had I known that there was a prior attachment in our dear boy's life and a feeling in his mind, I would never have bent down to breathe the scent of a flower intended for some other altar. He too would surely have warded off my first kiss if he had known that I was as good as married [to Mallefille – '*perfect* in respect of love and honour… the only man… who has surrendered to me completely and absolutely, without regret for the past or reservations for the future']. We did not deceive each other, we surrendered to the passing gale which carried us away for a while to another world. All the same, of course, we had to come back to earth when the divine flame had cooled and the journey through the empyrean blue had ended. We are like poor birds, who have wings indeed, but whose nest is on the ground, and while the song of angels beckons us heavenwards the cries of our nestlings bring us back to earth…

… pledged as I am… I cannot wish that our *dear boy* should for his part break the bonds which restrain him. Were he to come and place his life in my hands I should be greatly alarmed, for since I am responsible for another's happiness I could not take the place of someone *he* might have left for me. I feel that our love can only last in conditions such as those in which it was born, that is, that when from time to time a favourable breeze wafts us towards each other we should take a trip to the stars and then separate for the return to earth, for we are the children of Mother Earth and it is not God's will that we should follow our earthly pilgrimage side by side. Heaven is where we meet, and the fleeting moments we shall spend there will be so divine that they will equal a whole life spent in this vale of tears…

… I can, without forswearing myself, perform [my duty] in two distinct ways: the first would be to keep as far as possible from Chopin, to avoid trying to occupy his thoughts and never to find myself alone with him; the second would be to do the opposite and come as close as possible to him without causing Mallefille any misgivings. I could slip into his thoughts when he is at peace with the world, I could from time to time permit a chaste embrace whenever it pleased the wind of Heaven to lift us up and carry us to the skies. I shall adopt the first of these methods if the *young lady* is marked out to bring him happiness true and pure, to fulfil his every need, to order and tranquillise his life; if, in a word, she and only she is the one to ensure his happiness, while I could only be an obstacle to it.

If his spirit, which is *excessively*, perhaps *crazily* or perhaps wisely, scrupulous, will not allow itself to love two different beings in two different ways; if the one week that I may spend with him during each season is likely to prevent his being happy at home for the rest of the year then, yes, in that case I swear that I will do my best to make him forget me. I shall adopt the second method if you tell me one of two things: either that his domestic happiness can and must be achieved by means of a few hours of chaste passion and gentle poetry; or that happiness as a family man is out of the question for him and that marriage or any similar union would be the graveyard of this artist-soul, and that he must be kept from it at all costs and even be helped to overcome his religious scruples... I think that you dread marriage for him and the bonds of everyday life, real life, business matters, domestic cares, everything in fact which seems remote from his nature and contrary to the inspirations of his muse. I should dread it for him also; but I can make no pronouncement and can affirm nothing in the matter because in many respects I have no knowledge of him... You must therefore give me some precise information... Following my own preferences, I had thought out our romance along the following lines: that I should remain in complete ignorance of his *positive* life, as he should of mine; that he should keep to his own ideas on religion, fashionable society, poetry and art, without my ever having to call them into question and reciprocally; but that, wherever and on whatever occasion in our lives we happened to meet, our souls should be at the peak of their goodness and happiness. For I am convinced that one is a better human being when one loves with sublime emotion; and so far from committing any crime one rather draws near to God, the source and centre of this love. These are, perhaps, the things which you ought to try in the last resort to make him understand, my friend, and you could perhaps set his mind at rest without coming into conflict with his ideas of duty, devotion and religious sacrifice. What I should most dread and what would distress me most, what would make me resolve to be *dead for him*, would be to see myself become a source of terror and remorse in his soul…

If his heart can, like mine, contain two different loves, one which is so to speak the *body* of life while the other is the *soul*, so much the better, for then our position will be adapted to our feelings and thoughts. Just as one cannot be *sublime* every day, so one cannot be *happy* every day. We shall not see each other every day; every day we shall not be consumed by the sacred fire, but there will be *some* fine days and *some* holy flames…

So far I have been faithful to whomsoever I have loved, perfectly faithful in the sense that I have never deceived anyone and have never ceased to be faithful unless I had very strong reasons which, through another's fault, had killed my love. I am not of an inconstant nature. On the contrary, I am so used to giving my exclusive affection to one who loves me truly, so slow to take fire, so accustomed to living with men without reflecting that I am a woman, that I was rather disturbed and frightened at the effect this little person [Chopin] had on me. I still have not got over my amazement, and if I were very proud I should feel humiliated at allowing my heart to fall straight into infidelity just when my life seemed calm and settled for ever.

Two months ago [April] I said, 'There is no love without fidelity', and it is very certain that I no longer felt the same tenderness towards poor M[allefille] when I saw him again. It is certain that since he returned to Paris (you must have seen him) instead of impatiently awaiting his arrival and being sad when he is not there I suffer less and breathe more freely. [The uneasiness and gloom with which I have accepted the renewal of (his) caresses and the courage I have needed to hide the fact from him – all this is a warning to me.]…

… one may be more or less unfaithful, but when one has allowed one's soul to be invaded and when one has granted the simplest caress, urged to it by the feeling of love, the infidelity has already been committed and what follows is less serious, for he who has lost the heart has lost everything. Better to lose the body and keep the soul intact. Hence, as a matter of principle, I think that a total consecration of the new bond does little to aggravate the initial fault, but rather that the attachment may even become more human, more powerful and dominating after possession. That is quite probable and even certain. And so, when two persons wish to live together, they should not violate nature and truth by retreating from a complete union; but should they be compelled to live apart, the wisest thing for them and hence a duty and true virtue (which means sacrifice) is to abstain...

... it will cost me dear to see our angel suffer. He has so far shown great strength; but I am not a child. I could well observe that his human passion was making rapid strides and that it was time we kept apart. That is why, the night before I left, I did not wish to be left alone with him and I practically turned you both out of doors...

... he displeased me by one single thing – the fact that he had had in his own mind the wrong reasons for abstaining. Until that moment I had considered it a fine thing that he abstained out of respect for me, out of shyness, even out of fidelity to another. There was an element of sacrifice in all that, and hence strength and chastity, as properly understood. It was that which charmed and allured me the most in him. But at your house, just as he was leaving us, and as if to overcome a final temptation, he said two or three words which did not at all correspond to my ideas. He seemed to despise (in the manner of a religious prude) the coarser side of human nature and to blush for temptations he had had, and to fear to soil our love by a further ecstasy. I have always loathed this way of looking at the final embrace of love. If this last embrace is not something as holy, as pure and as sacrificial as the rest, no virtue lies in abstaining from it. This phrase, 'physical love', which is used to convey the idea of something whose name is known only in Heaven, *displeases* and *shocks* me as being at once a blasphemy and a false idea. Can there be for lofty natures a purely physical love, and for sincere natures a love which is purely intellectual? Can there ever be love without a single kiss, and a kiss of love without sensual pleasure? *To scorn the flesh* can only have a wise and useful meaning for creatures who are nothing but *flesh*; but when two people love each other it is not the word *scorn* but *respect* that should be used when they abstain… He said, I think, that 'certain actions' might spoil our memories. It was foolish of him to say that, wasn't it? And can he mean it? Tell me, what wretched woman has left him with such impressions of physical love?… *

'*She* – beautiful auburn hair falling to her shoulders; eyes rather lustreless and sleepy, but calm and gentle; a smile of great good nature; a somewhat dead, somewhat husky voice, difficult to hear, for George is far from talkative, and takes in a great deal more than she gives out. *He* – endowed with abnormal sensitiveness which the least contact can wound, on which the tiniest sound will strike like thunder: a man made for intimacies, withdrawn into a mysterious world of his own, from which he sometimes emerges in a sudden spate or violent, charming and fantastic speech' (Heine). *He* – treading beyond his comfort zone: 'God knows what will come of it. I am really not well' he confides to Grzymała in early July, about to see her at the Marlianis having spent a day, 'like a stone', teaching. *She* – happy to nurture, comfort and inspire, to live by her free feelings. Following a summer spent largely in each other's embrace, 'nothing,' she tells Delacroix – who's been sketching them for a joint portrait† – 'gives such languor in the bones as the delicious lassitude that flows from happy love. I remain in the intoxication in which you saw me last… I am beginning to believe that angels can appear disguised as men, dwelling for some time upon the earth, in order to console and lure heavenwards behind them poor, exhausted and troubled souls, close to ruin. If in one hour's time God were to send me death, I would not complain, as three months have passed in undisturbed intoxication' (7 September).

* Translated Arthur Hedley. In his Sand biography, Maurois remarks that this letter has been 'severely criticised. Indignation – and sometimes amusement – has been expressed, because, in the course of it, Sand spoke frankly of matters which most people, then as now, might think but not put into words. To hypocrites all sincerity has the appearance of cynicism'.

† Subsequently divided, Chopin's image (right side, *see* frontispiece, p.6) hangs in the Louvre, Sand's in the Ordrupgård, Charlottenlund.

El Mallorquin (The Majorcan) -
the first steam-assisted ship to
the Balearic Islands - sailing past
the signal tower of Faro de Porto Pi
and arriving at Palma.

9. Mallorca

'… sketches, the beginnings of studies… ruins, eagle's feathers…'

Robert Schumann on the Préludes

Lives changed, nearly ended, that autumn and winter of '38. Having published, within hours of Sand's rapturous admission, a eulogistic piece on Poland and Chopin in the *Revue et Gazette Musicale de Paris* (9 September) – 'as proof of my affection for you and my sympathy for your heroic country' – then realising his naivety, the cuckolded Mallefille, with 'the hot passions of a [Mauritian] Créole' (Maurois), attempted to shoot George and/or challenge Fryderyk to a duel (accounts differ). 'Scandal and violence,' to be made 'the laughing-stock of his elegant friends in the Faubourg Saint-Germain', wasn't part of Chopin's agenda. Needing to de-fuse the situation, Sand proposed a spell in Mallorca. Her Spanish intimates, unfamiliar though they were with the place, enthused that it would be 'an ideal spot for sunshine and fresh air, for writing, studying and love-making' (Hedley). Chopin's were less convinced. 'Consumption has taken possession of his face'… 'he is following her to Spain [...] he will never leave that country' (Astolphe de Custine). She, young Solange and the rheumatic Maurice, together with her maid, Amélie, left Paris on 18 October, heading for Perpignan in the Pyrénées-Orientales. Borrowing 2,000 francs from Pleyel in exchange for the as yet unfinished *Préludes,* Chopin set off shortly afterwards, arriving on the 31st – 'fresh as a daisy and as red as a beetroot,' according to Sand in a letter to Carlotta Marliani, 'in good health, after four nights heroically spent in a mail-coach'.

Perpignan was a sleepy town, crowned by the *basilique-cathédrale* of St. John the Baptist and a medieval castle that in the 13th and 14th centuries had been the mainland palace and citadel of the Kingdom of Mallorca. The atmosphere was unique: Chopin hadn't sensed such adventure and new worlds since his first journeys away from Poland. At five o'clock on the evening of Wednesday 7th November, having travelled down the Mediterranean coast to Barcelona, the lovers boarded the steam-schooner *El Mallorquin*, formally registered as 'Mme. Dudevant [George Sand], married [*sic*]; M. Maurice, her son, minor; Mlle. Solange, her daughter, minor, and M. Fryderyk Chopin, artist'. In her diary Sand left an atmospheric description of the voyage to Palma:

> The night was warm and dark, illuminated only by an extraordinary phosphorescence in the wake of the ship; everybody was asleep on board, except the steersman, who, in order to keep himself awake, sang all night, but in a voice so soft and subdued that one might have thought that he feared to awake the men of the watch, or that he himself was half asleep. We did not weary of listening to him, for his singing was of the strangest kind. He observed a rhythm and modulation totally different from those we are accustomed to, and seemed to allow his voice to go at random, like the smoke of the vessel carried away and swayed by the breeze. It was a reverie rather than a song, a kind of careless floating of the voice, with which the mind had little to do, but which kept time with the swaying of the ship, the faint sound of the dark water, and resembled a vague improvisation, restrained nevertheless by sweet and monotonous forms.

Palma was a quiet, romantic spot. The sea met with long stretches of beach, while the harbour walls sheltered a bay dominated by a towering cathedral set against a backcloth of receding hills. Mallorca was the largest of the Balearic Islands in the western Mediterranean, under Spanish sovereignty since the 13th century. A trading-post from pre-historic times, the island had offered refuge to the Phoenicians, Greeks, Carthaginians, Romans, Vandals and Byzantines, all of whom left evidence of their occupation. Later, the Moors arrived, the place becoming a hideaway for Barbary pirates – Moslem seafarers preying the Christian shipping lanes. Massive Cyclopean remains lifted the landscape, put there, the stories go, by the one-eyed giants of Greek mythology: 'a fierce, uncivilised people,' Homer chronicled, 'who... have no assemblies for the making of laws, nor any settled customs, but live in hollow caverns in the mountain heights, where each man is lawgiver to his children and his wives, and nobody cares anything for his neighbours'.

The beauties of the island were unspoilt and uninvaded.

Palma: lithograph from Jean-Joseph-Bonaventure Laurens' *Souvenirs d'un voyage d'art à l'île de Majorque* (Paris, Montpellier 1840).

The inhabitants were mostly poor, scratching a living from wine-making and the rearing of sheep and pigs; or from mining marble and copper. They followed a closed life-style their forefathers would have recognised centuries earlier. They offered no welcome to strangers.

Some rooms were rented above a barrel-maker's workshop, offering a noisy contrast to the luxuries of Paris. Chopin's and Sand's new-found freedom and involvement with one other made them oblivious to such conditions. Sand was in a gay mood, writing after a week (13 November):

> When you arrive here you begin by buying a piece of land, then you build a house and order the furniture. After that you obtain the government's permission to live somewhere and finally at the end of five or six years [!] you begin to open your luggage and change your shirt, while awaiting permission from the customs to import shoes and handkerchiefs.

The Villa son Vent: drawing by Maurice Dudevant-Sand.

A few days later, on the 19th, Chopin posted an enthusiastic letter to Fontana. Communications were so slow and unpredictable however (there was just a weekly mail-boat) that it only reached Paris after Christmas:

> I am in Palma, among palms, cedars, cacti, olives, pomegranates, etc. Everything the *Jardin des Plantes* [the botanical gardens in Paris, on the Left Bank] has in its greenhouses. A sky like turquoise, a sea like lapis lazuli, mountains like emerald, air like heaven. Sun all day, and hot; everyone in summer clothing; at night guitars and singing for hours. Huge balconies with grape-vines overhead; Moorish walls. Everything looks towards Africa, as the town does. In short, a glorious life! Love me. Go to Pleyel: the piano has not yet come. How was it sent? You will soon receive some *Préludes*. I shall probably lodge in a wonderful monastery, the most beautiful situation in the world: sea, mountains, palms, a cemetery, a crusader's church, ruined mosques, aged trees, thousand-year-old olives. Ah, my dear, I am coming alive a little. I am near to what is most beautiful. I am better.

'Villa son Vent', The House of the Wind', a villa in

Establiments, a village near Palma, was the couple's next home – a small, plain white-washed, square, primitively furnished building with shuttered windows and a flight of crumbling steps (15 November-9 December). The weather, like Paris in summer, proved a tonic for Chopin's constitution. Enjoying long country walks with Sand and the children, he one day headed for a lonely spot on the seashore which could only be reached by a rough goat track leading down the craggy cliff face. On the way home, a violent gale blew in from the sea, buffeting him so much that his lungs became weakened. Arguably it was the turning point of his life, for he never really recovered. His bronchitis, coupled with the poor living conditions, became magnified when the weather deteriorated further and winter suddenly arrived. Torrential rains nearly flooded the villa, the bare plaster walls were swollen with rising damp, and a dank, fungus-smelling chill settled over everything. A charcoal stove, overpowering in its fumes, was the sole protection against the elements. Chopin's cough grew worse. In a letter, written to Fontana from Palma (3 December), he sketches his predicament – with remarkable humour given the circumstances:

> I have been as sick as a dog these last two weeks; I caught cold in spite of 18 degrees of heat, roses, oranges, palms, figs and three most famous doctors of the island. One sniffed at what I spat up, the second tapped where I spat it from, the third poked about and listened to how I spat it. One said I had kicked the bucket, the second that I am dying, the third that I shall die… […] *grâce à la Providence* I am today back to normal.

Rumours of tuberculosis spread through the village, with the owner of the villa demanding exorbitant compensation and a costly disinfection for his apparently 'soiled' summer house. Conditions for Chopin and Sand had suddenly become desperate, particularly as their future rooms in the old, abandoned Carthusian monastery at Valldemossa (to the north) were not yet ready to occupy. This late 14th century former 'royal residence' was an isolated, silent place, set among thickly forested mountains, and Sand and Chopin had come across it during one of their early trips around the island. Three years previously the last monks had been disbanded by government order. The cells opened out into a small, walled garden, wild and overgrown, below which, stretching down the valley,

Julian Fontana (1810–69): bronze medallion by Władisław Oleszczyński, 1843.

were terraces of vineyards and orange and almond trees. The surrounding mountains curved together in a protective wall, only broken to the south by a gap through which the waters of the Mediterranean could be seen on a clear day. Swayed by it all, Sand had been seduced (15 November):

I have… reserved a cell, *ie* three rooms and a <u>garden</u>, for thirty-five francs a year [£100 in today's money] in the monastery of Valldemossa—a huge and splendid deserted convent in the mountains. Our garden is strewn with oranges and lemons: the trees are cracking beneath their burden… Vast cloisters of the most beautiful architecture, a delightful church, a cemetery with a palm tree and a stone cross like the one in the third act of *Robert le Diable* [Meyerbeer's opera]. The only inhabitants of the place, besides ourselves, are an old serving-woman and the sacristan—our steward, door-keeper and *major-domo* rolled into one. I hope we shall have some ghosts. My cell

The Monastery at Valldemossa: drawing by Bartolomé Ferrá, 1930.

The Cemetry at Valldemossa: drawing by George Sand, 1839.

door looks on to a huge cloister, and when the wind slams the door, it rumbles like gunfire through the convent. You see that I shall not lack poetry and solitude.

It was arranged for Sand and Chopin to take over the rooms and furniture (from a Spanish political refugee and his wife) on 15 December. Chopin remained sick – notwithstanding Sand's assertion the day before that 'he is recovering, and I hope he will soon be better than before. His goodness and patience are angelic. We are so different from most of the people and things around us... our family ties are only more strengthened by it and we cling to each other with more affection and intimate happiness.'

Moving to Valldemossa was something neither Sand nor Chopin seem to have given much thought to. Certainly it was romantic. But it was also a place exposed to high winds and bad weather. Clinging, rain-laden mists rolled in from the sea, and the sun rarely emerged from behind the winter clouds, save occasionally late in the morning. Notwithstanding a lack of food and creature comforts, Chopin seemed taken with the surroundings. A few days after Christmas he wrote to Fontana:

Palma, 28 Dec[ember] 1838… or rather Valldemossa, a few miles away. It's a huge Carthusian monastery, between the rocky cliffs and the sea, where you may imagine me without gloves or haircurling, as pale as ever, in a cell with such doors as Paris never had for gates. The cell* is the shape of a tall coffin, with an enormous dusty vaulting, a small window; outside the window, orange trees, palms and cypresses opposite the window, my bed on straps under a Moorish filigree rosette. Beside the bed is a square and soiled writing desk [*claque nitouchable*], which I can scarcely use, and on it (a great luxury here) a leaden candle-stick with a candle. Bach, my scrawls, and another's waste-paper; silence, you could scream, and there would still be silence. Indeed, I write to you from a strange place… Nature is benevolent here, but the people are thieves because they never see strangers and so don't know how much to demand. Oranges can be bought for nothing, but a trouser button costs a fabulous sum. But all that is just a grain of sand when one has this sky, this poetry that everything breathes here, this colouring of the most exquisite places, colour not yet faded by men's eyes. No one has yet scared away the eagles that soar every day above our heads!

Sand worked on a new novel, *Spiridion* – 'a far-ahead-of-its-time work about a haunted monastery, an aged monk who is the guardian of handed-down religious secrets, a young, innocent protégé, ghosts emerging from paintings on the ancient walls' (Tina Kover). And taught the children. Wild as the birds, they revelled in their new playground. Maurice was fond of sketching and left many drawings of the monastery, its gardens and cemetery, and the surrounding countryside. In maternal mode, Sand kept a goat for milk, prepared the meals, and generally tried to create a home. Occasionally she joined the children on their rambles, and was once seen at the theatre in Palma. Secure that she was near to him, Chopin composed. His health made it impossible to leave the monastery, however, and he grew more and more morbid and disturbed when left alone. By mid-winter, Sand says, Valldemossa had become for him a place of predatory, ever-lurking terrors and phantoms.

When she and Chopin opted to visit Mallorca, one of their intentions had been to further their artistic horizons. Almost every factor challenged them. Chopin's plan to write new works

* *Which* one specifically has been the object of two feuding families since the 1930s, unresolved until a Palma court judgement early in 2011 (*Daily Telegraph*, 1 February 2011; *Süddeutsche Zeitung*, 26 October 2011).

Valldemossa, 1840: lithograph from
Souvenirs d'un voyage d'art à l'île de Majorque.

was only realised partially. Held up in transit, his Pleyel didn't arrive until mid-January (1839), forcing him to use an inferior local upright. Still, he managed to finalise the *Préludes*, sending them to Fontana on 22 January, asking him to give them personally to Pleyel. Though most of the twenty-four date from earlier, several were written on the island, two (the A minor, No. 2 and E minor, No. 4) sketched at the end of November – the time Chopin was taken ill. If there are moments in Chopin's music when every note would seem a silvered glass to his most poignant tensions, then such *préludes* would surely have to qualify. (The E minor was played at his funeral service.)

'The rain came in overflowing torrents... We got back in absolute dark, shoeless, having been abandoned by our driver to cross unheard of perils'. Within, Chopin was playing one of his *préludes* to the monotonous accompaniment of rain dripping from the eaves. 'When I called his attention to those drops of water... he denied having heard them. He was even vexed at what I translated by the term, 'mimetic harmony'. He protested with all his might – and he was right – against the puerility of these imitations for the ear. His genius was full of the mysterious harmonies of nature... [resounding raindrops] transformed in imagination and song into tears falling upon his heart from the

* Publicly, Chopin resisted the notion of stories or extra-musical impulses behind his work: contrasting Liszt, Henselt, Schumann, a whole host of contemporaries, he revealed practically nothing to appease Romantic curiosity. Privately, however, his undated sketches for a piano *Méthode* (Piermont Morgan Library, New York) suggest that music to him was more than simply a set of abstract parameters, that it was a medium through which could be voiced the narrative of the senses and the unspoken. 'Thought expressed through sounds'. 'The expression of our perceptions through sounds'. 'The manifestation of our feelings through sounds'. 'The indefinite (indeterminate) language of men is sound'. 'Word is born of sound – sound before word'. Thought, perception, feeling. Sound as the carrier, the barometer, of a man's emotions, his calm and angst, his loves, despairs and spiritual states.

sky' (*Histoire de ma vie*) *. What Sand heard, a minority have proposed, was No. 6, the 'cello' B minor, with its deliberated pulse and repeated notes in the upper right hand part. Most, however, favour No. 15, the 'Greco-Gothic' D flat. Here the same quaver tone (A flat/G sharp) sounds from beginning to end, a baroque fantasy on one note passing through an oppressive procession of images. 'The shades of the dead monks seem to rise and pass before the listener in solemn and gloomy funeral pomp' (Sand). 'What melancholy raindrops falling one by one on the tiles in the cell garden!' (Solange).

With fleeting exceptions – the short-lived B flat *Prélude* (No. 22), a ray of sunshine piercing dark clouds – Chopin's Mallorcan music was melancholic, and more than once obsessed with repetitious motifs or accompaniments. 'Morbid' was how Victorians liked to describe it. The tragic face of the Polonaise in C minor, Op. 40 No. 2, its bass theme echoing and transmoding Kurpiński's 1825 D major *Coronation* Polonaise, the Russian composer-pianist Anton Rubinstein likened to the downfall of Poland. Correspondence with Fontana, the dedicatee, 7 March 1839, implies an unspecified extra-musical dimension: 'you will find an answer to your sincere and genuine letter in the second Polonaise'. Other storm winds gust across the C sharp minor Scherzo (No. 3), begun in January 1839 and finished that summer, inscribed to the composer's pupil, Adolf Gutmann – a Heidelberg bruiser given to 'knocking a hole in the table' with the first left-hand chord. In a hell versus the pulpit scenario, from chromatic exclamation to diatonic exorcism, its pages oppose turbulent 'demon' images with placatory chorales and cascading showers of 'water' notes.

The incidents and artefacts, the pen-and-inks and *dramatis personæ*, of this rain-drenched winter have long passed into Romantic lore. 2,330 hours. The wan, unshaven, hollow-cheeked Chopin of the 'black heart', surrounded by squalor, coughing blood by the bucketful, possessed by 'ghosts and horrors'. The modest Pleyel *pianino* sent from Paris. Maurice and his sketchbook, recording the surroundings. The petulant, scheming, 'idolised' Solange, all of ten but a 'rebellious, arrogant, lazy […] domestic tyrant who relied on violent displays of temper for getting her own way' (Robert Graves). *Préludes*, *Spiridion*. The 'harpies' and huntsmen of the hills, the demon landlord, the local priest aghast at Sand's life-choices. 'Just think of it,' Karol Dembowski, a January visitor, reports this man saying. 'She never speaks to a living soul, never leaves the *cartuja*, and never shows her face in church, not even on Sundays, and goodness only knows how many mortal sins she is amassing! […] *la señora* makes cigarettes like nothing on earth, drinks coffee at all hours, sleeps by day, and does nothing but smoke and write at night'. 'On Mallorca we were pariahs, due

Genoa. 'To see the Genoese and to know them, to realise their character, and the things which make up the sum of their existence, you must climb up the stairways which do duty for streets, or go down the maze of side alleys near the Piazzo di Sarzana behind the old wall: streets so narrow that you may touch the houses on both sides as you pass ... Over the miserable little doorways you will see lordly coats of arms cut in black marble, and squatting on the doorsteps you will find such of the adult population as inhabit the ground floor, while those who live up the dark and broken stairs lean out among the washing to gape and chatter ... pervading all is the odour of things of the sea mixed with that of incense and eatables' – Robert W. Carden, 1908.

to Chopin's cough, and also because we did not attend Mass. Stones were thrown at my children. They said we were pagans' (Sand to Countess Marliani, 15 February 1839). Her bitter monograph, *Un hiver à Majorque*, voicing her 'insensate rage against the islanders' (Graves), only provoked locals to have the last word. 'George Sand is the most immoral of writers, and Mme Dudevant the most obscene of women' (Don José Quadrado, *La Palma*, 5 May 1841).

To flee this 'complete fiasco' was imperative. Travelling the rough road to Palma in 'a hired cart without springs', Chopin 'began to spit blood terribly; the next day [13 February] we got on [the *El Mallorquin*] the only steamboat running from the island, which transports pigs to Barcelona… The endless squealing and hideous stench prevented the patient from resting or drawing fresh air. He sailed into Barcelona having spat out a bowl-full of blood and reeling like a ghost' (Sand). Transferred to a French brig and given a week of medical care in Barcelona, Chopin, a wreck of the former happy adventurer, and Sand made their way to 'ugly' industrial Marseilles, arriving on the 24th. Here he recovered quickly, his correspondence, especially to Fontana, revealing again an alert, selectively choosy, business mind.

Albeit living 'in the clouds… his life or death mean nothing to him… he is unaware of what planet he is living on' (Sand to Marliani, 26 April), Chopin tried to share Sand's life more fully. He encouraged her to take an interest in Polish literature, and translated Mickiewicz for her. In the enthusiasm of the moment she penned an *Essai sur le drame fantastique: Goethe, Byron, Mickiewicz* (published in December in *Revue des deux mondes*), which he declared to be 'magnificent… one must read it. It gladdens the heart.'

Preferring to keep his presence in Marseilles private, Chopin made just one public appearance – on 24 April at a memorial service for his friend Adolphe Nourrit, the French tenor who in a state of delirium, following a poor concert the night before, had committed suicide on 8 March. During May (3rd-18th), he and Sand went on a sea excursion to Genoa, a place with memories for her who'd eloped there in 1833 with de Musset. From Marseilles, leaving on the 22nd, the pair journeyed quietly to Nohant – via ship to Arles, then coach through St. Étienne, Montbrison and Clermont-Ferrand – arriving on June 1st, to be among companions again, and to soak in the warmth and indolence, the inimitable Frenchness, of Berry rurality. The years at Nohant, the high-point of Chopin's art, were to be his enduring swan song.

Nohant, where Chopin spent seven
summers and wrote the finest music
of his life.

10. Nohant

'Light clouds take on all the forms of fantasy; they fill the sky; they crowd round the moon which casts upon them large opal discs, awakening their dormant colours. We dream of a summer night: we await the nightingale. A sublime melody arises'

George Sand

The Garden of France. 'There are none of the things [here one fears]: no spying, no gossip, no provincial neighbours; it's an oasis in the desert. There's not a soul for miles around who knows what a Chopin or a Grzymała is. No one knows what goes on in my house. I see only intimate friends, darlings like you, who have never thought any evil of those whom they love' (Sand to Grzymała, June 1838).

Nohant's Louis XVI-style *château* and estate enchanted Chopin. The peaceful surroundings – a locale variously reflected in Sand's writings – must have been a welcome salvation from the nightmare of Mallorca.

> It was a plain, handsome [three-storey] manor house without pretension: the main gates faced the village square and the garden, at that season scented with white lilac, was informal. Imperfectly standardised shrubs stood in tubs on the terrace; shaggy archways of vine bordered the lawn; an old tower housed the flock of noisy doves. A farm belonged also to the property, and woods abounding in wild strawberries; nearby flowed the Indre, one of those ravishing miniature rivers that bind the landscape of central France like so many ribbons *.

Friends left aromatic recollections. Delacroix (7 June 1842): 'This is a delightful place... every now and then there blows in through your window – opening on to the garden – a breath of the music of Chopin who is at work in his room, and it mingles with the song of the nightingales, and the scent of roses.' In her *Memoirs* Marie d'Agoult remembered 'a promenade along the Indre [a tributary of the Loire], the length of the woody path, across the meadows covered with forget-me-nots, nettles

*Eleanor Perényi, *Liszt: the artist as romantic hero* (New York 1974). See also Bernadette Pécassou-Camebrac, *Invitation chez George Sand* (DVD: Artline Films/France 3 co-production [2006])

and English daisies, climbing many rustic fences, meeting with families of geese and herds of cattle majestically ruminating...'

At first the time spent *en famille* at Nohant was idyllic. Sand had Chopin's study sound-proofed. He found the village, between the Paris Basin and *massif central*, 'beautiful', its nightingales and skylarks lending their own music to the hours of sun, dusk and stars. 'A quiet, gentle life. We eat dinner in the open air. Our friends comes to see us, now one, now another. We smoke and chat, and in the evening when they have gone, Chopin plays to me... after which he goes to bed like a child' (Sand, 15 June 1839).

Chopin found the will to compose again. That summer of 1839, having spent the spring haggling with publishers – 'about whom he never ceases to complain and whom he reviles without restraint' (Tomaszewski) – he worked on the Second Sonata seeded from the 1837 Funeral March; the Mediterraneanesque Nocturne in G major (Op. 37 No. 2), completed in July; the F sharp major Impromptu; and the Op. 41 Mazurkas. Away in Leipzig Schumann favourably reviewed the Op. 33 Mazurkas, Op. 34 Waltzes, and *Préludes*, noting that in spite of their 'colourful and chaotic mixture [each] is marked in his pearly hand: "written by Fryderyk Chopin"; one recognizes him from the breathless pauses' (*Neue Zeitschrift für Musik*, 19 July). Like Mendelssohn ('I abhor it'), he was less enamoured, however, with the Sonata when it was published in May 1840 ('largely repulsive'). Celebrated by Liszt, re-angled by Anton Rubinstein, piano-rolled by Hofmann, recorded by Rachmaninov, rhetorized by Cortot ('terror weighs upon this work like a tragic question addressed to Destiny'), this commands as Romanticism's toughest display of cyclic-ordering in the period between Schubert's *Wanderer* and Alkan's *Quasi-Faust*. Its DNA is about one interval – the minor third. From the *grave/doppio movimento* of the opening movement... to the finale's 'gossiping' tornado of crazily tumbling wraiths, hands locked at the octave. From the E flat minor scherzo and Beethovenian thrust... to the *marche funèbre* and music of paternally old rhythms and *minore* lament, falling melodies and *maggiore* solace, death symbols and *requiem* flight.

The impending closure of Nohant for the winter (in the event twenty-one months, 1840 being spent in Paris) and plans to return to the capital called for Chopin to be at his most exacting. Entrusting his business affairs and domestic needs to Fontana, *mon chéri*, he asks for a hat and new clothes. 'Dupont in your

Eugène Delacroix (1798-1863) self-portrait, 1837. 'Talent does whatever it wants to do... Genius does only what it can'. 'A volcanic crater artistically concealed beneath bouquets of flowers' – Charles Baudelaire.

street... has my measurements, and knows how light I need them. Let him give me this year's fashion, not exaggerated. Also go in, as you pass, to Dautremont, my tailor on the boulevard, and tell him to make me a pair of grey trousers at once. You can choose a shade of dark grey; winter trousers, good quality, without belt, smooth and stretchy... Also a plain black velvet waistcoat, but with a tiny inconspicuous pattern – something very quiet and elegant' (postmarked La Châtre, 4 October).

Searching out apartments to rent, Fontana has to comply with a demanding set of criteria and localities. Fryderyk is precise and calm as to how he wants his place furnished and draped. George is fussy, repetitious, even paranoid. 'It must be quite, private, no blacksmith nearby, no girls [of the night], etc, etc. You understand perfectly... Well exposed to sunlight, facing south... No bad smells. Fairly high. No smoke; light, as attractive as possible; that is to say: a pleasant outlook, to a garden or a large courtyard by preference... Find it like lightning, by inspiration; something splendid' (October, undated). Arriving in Paris, 11 October, he takes over (damp, sunless cough-inducing) rooms at 5 rue Tronchet, *arrondissement* 6*, on the Right Bank. George and her two children – Maurice the aspiring artist taking lessons from 'Lacroix' (Delacroix); the boudoir-preoccupied Solange, 'fresh as a rosebud and extremely intelligent' – are forced to wait until January, however, before settling in at 16 rue Pigalle in Montmartre... 'having' for weeks, she says, 'fumed, raged, stormed, and sworn at the upholsterers, locksmith, etc., etc. What a long, horrible, unbearable business it is to lodge one's self here!' Few strangers penetrated their secret. Even Chopin's parents, if curious, did not appear to suspect anything deeper than a close friendship.

Teaching (at rue Tronchet, from 11 in the morning, at 30 francs a lesson), seeing through Opp. 35-42 to Paris, Leipzig and London publication, a high-status social calendar, and sparodic composition (more or less in that order) occupied Chopin until returning to Nohant in June 1841. Old masters, piano pioneers, and the new school coloured his pupils' repertory. Bach, Beethoven... Cramer, Hummel, Moscheles... Field, Liszt, Thalberg... his own works. Finely-graced 'heavenly misses' made up his wealthiest pupils. But, following in the footsteps of Gutmann (from 1834), there were also aspiring new stars. Notably the Kalkbrenner-schooled Georges Mathias (1838/39 through much of the forties); and Friederike Müller from Moravia (1839-41). 'Among the *coryphées* of her art' (*Revue et Gazette Musicale*, 1 May 1842), 'one of Chopin's best professional students' (Eigeldinger), it was Müller who played the Second Sonata at a private *soirée* in 1840 (20 December). The following year Chopin dedicated the *Allegro de Concert* to her.

'I do not see Chopin at all. He is wallowing in the aristocratic mire up to his ears. he is refined to the highest degree... He prefers high salons to high mountains, the stifling fumes of gaslight to clean mountain air' (Heller to Schumann, 4 January

1840). Blue-bloods, artistic, literary, musical and theatrical luminaries, the blazing comets of the metropolis, stamped the Chopin-Sand set. Balzac, Berlioz, the Marquis de Custine back from Russia and Siberia, the Czartoryski circle, Delacroix, Dorval, Grzymała, Gutmann, Hugo, Lamartine, Leroux, Liszt, Mickiewicz, Sainte-Beuve, Viardot, Witwicki… Attending concerts, the theatre, and public lectures together, neither seemed especially bothered to hide their liaison. 'She comes with the famous pianist Chopin and leaves in his carriage,' comments an observer in January 1841. Two months later, describing her salon, with its 'magnificent Chinese vases [and] splendid ['upright square'] piano of Brazilian rosewood,' Balzac says matter-of-factly 'Chopin is always here'.

Towards the end of 1839 Chopin re-established contact with Moscheles, to whom he played the new Second Sonata. The response was warm. A few days later they duetted together, Chopin *secondo*, for the French court at the Château de Saint-Cloud. In addition to being a noted pianist, conductor, composer and writer, Moscheles, a staunch Beethovenian, was also the editor – together with Fétis – of a *Méthode des Méthodes de Piano ou Traité de l'art de jouer de cet instrument*, Op. 98, the final volume of which, published in Paris and Berlin in November 1840 (but proofed as early as January), comprised twenty *études de perfectionnement* commissioned from different composers. Chopin's *Trois [nouvelles] études* joined a *Morceau de salon* by Liszt and Mendelssohn's 1836 Étude in F minor, as well as studies by Henselt, Hiller and Thalberg.

1840 was spent in the capital, mainly because George Sand's play, *Cosima*, produced at the Comédie-Française in April with Marie Dorval in the title rôle, had failed, and she couldn't afford to live at Nohant or invite guests for the summer. Aside from aristocratic *bijouterie* – like the A flat Waltz, Op. 42 ('a salon piece of the noblest kind,' viewed Schumann, 'half of the ladies should be countesses at least' – Paris didn't encourage Chopin to compose anything large-scale, and it wasn't until the autumn/winter of 1840–41 that he sketched the F sharp minor Polonaise, Op. 44 ('a kind of polonaise, but more of a fantasy') and Third Ballade – works in the epic vein of the B flat minor Sonata. Both were finished at Nohant during the summer of 1841. The more seering was the polonaise, about which Liszt wrote:

> … the central section could be likened to the first glimmer of a winter dawn, dull and grey, the tale of a dream after

a sleepless night, a dream-poem where impressions and objects unfold with strange incoherencies and strange transitions… The principal motive of the polonaise itself has an ominous air, like the hour before the hurricane; desperate exclamations seem to fall upon the ear, a defiance hurled at all the elements…

The Fantasy in F minor was finalised a little later, an example of Chopin's art at its most resoundingly epic. 'Today I finished the Fantasy – a beautiful sky, a sadness in my heart – but that is all right. If it were otherwise, perhaps my existence would be worth nothing to anyone. Let us hide until death has passed' (Nohant, 20 October 1841).

Socially, 1840 was generally uneventful – highlighted at the start (January) by a visit to the Théâtre-Française to see the *tragédienne* Rachel Félix, mistress to many, in Racine's *Bajazet*, accompanied by Sand and de Lamennais; and at the end (December) by Mickiewicz's course of lectures on Slavonic literature at the Collège de France.

The tenth anniversary of the July 1830 Revolution passed with a ceremony during which the remains of the patriots were re-interred beneath the July Column in the Place de la Bastille. To mark the occasion, Berlioz, dislike of the régime notwithstanding, was commissioned by the government to write his *Grande symphonie funèbre et triomphale,* a rehearsal of which Chopin and Sand attended on 26 July, two days before the official unfurling. Scored for a military band of 200 (the closing chorus, like the work's title, was added later), conceived for open air performance, here was music of the very grandest pomp and ceremonial. In his *Memoirs,* Berlioz said that he wished to 'recall the famous Three Days' conflict amid the mournful accents of a solemn march accompanying the procession; to follow this by a sort of funeral oration [trombone solo], or farewell address to the illustrious dead, while the bodies were being lowered into the tomb; and finally to sing a hymn of praise as an apotheosis when, after the sealing of the tomb, the attention should be concentrated on the column alone, surmounted by the figure of Liberty, with her wings outstretched to heaven, like the souls of those who had died for her.'

On 29 November the body of Napoléon (whose nephew, Louis Napoléon Bonaparte – later Napoléon III – had tried earlier that year to seize power, only to be imprisoned for his failure) arrived back in France from St. Helena, where he'd died in exile in May 1821. A state funeral, from the Arc de Triomphe along the Champs-Élysées to the Esplanade des Invalides and then St. Jérôme's Chapel, followed on 15 December, Mozart's *Requiem* featuring in the proceedings, a work heard infrequently in the Paris of those days. Chopin and Sand were at the rehearsal on the 12th.

A few months later, on 26 April, the day after Liszt's *Emperor* with Berlioz at the Conservatoire, Chopin gave a semi-private concert at the Salle Pleyel, 22 rue de Rochechouart, before a selected gathering of aristocracy, friends, and pupils – including Liszt, Mickiewicz and Witwicki – who paid as much as 20 francs for each ticket (around £60 in modern currency). George Sand: 'He wants no posters, no programmes, no large audience, and wants nothing to be said on the subject. So many things frighten him that I have proposed that he play without candles and without the auditorium on a mute piano'. 'In two hours of two-handed tapping he pocketed six thousand and several hundred francs amidst ovations, encores and the stamping of the most beautiful women in Paris'. 6,000 francs… compared with 20-30 for a lesson, or around 500 for a composition – 'a price below which I shall provide nothing' (to the German publisher Breitkopf & Härtel, 14 December 1839). Following the fashion, he shared his 'Mallorcan' programme – with the soprano Laure Cinti-Damoreau, one of the *bel canto* stars of the Paris stage, and the violinist Heinrich Wilhelm Ernst, who as a young virtuoso was known for imitating the peculiarities of Paganini. Chopin received a brilliant reception, the editor of *La France Musicale* writing:

> Chopin is a composer from conviction. He composes for himself and performs for himself… In truth nothing equals the lightness, the sweetness with which this artist preludes on the piano; moreover nothing can be placed beside his works, full of originality, distinction and grace. Chopin is a pianist apart, who should not be and cannot be compared with anyone.

The most exotic, not to say gushing, write-up came, however, from Liszt in *La Gazette Musicale* (2 May 1841). This chose to concentrate less on Chopin, more on the glamour, the social air and atmosphere, of the occasion:

> Last Monday evening at eight o'clock the salons of

Hector Berlioz (1803–69): after the drawing by August Prinzhofer, Vienna 1845.

M[onsieur] Pleyel were brilliantly lighted; a ceaseless stream of carriages deposited at the foot of the steps, carpeted and decked with fragrant flowers, the most elegant ladies, the most fashionable young men, the most famous artists, the richest financiers, the most illustrious lords, the élite of society—a complete aristocracy of birth, wealth, talent and beauty.

An open grand piano was on the platform; crowding around, people vied for the closest seats; composing themselves in anticipation, they would not miss a chord, a note, an intention, a thought of him who was about to sit there. And they were right to be so greedy, attentive, and religiously wrought up, for the one they waited for, the one they wanted to see, hear, admire, and applaud was not only a skilled virtuoso, a pianist expert in the playing of notes—he was not only an artist of great renown—he was all this and much more, he was Chopin.

… In Monday's concert Chopin had chosen by preference those of his works farthest removed from the classical forms. He played neither concerto nor sonata, nor fantasy, nor variations, but *préludes, études,* nocturnes and mazurkas. Speaking to a society rather than to a public, he could safely show himself as what he is: a poet, elegiac, profound, chaste and dreaming. He had no need to astonish or to shock; he sought delicate sympathy rather than noisy acclaim. Let us say at once that this sympathy was not lacking. With the very first chords he established an intimate communication between himself and his audience. Two *études* and a ballade [No. 2] had to be repeated, and but for fear of increasing the fatigue already obviously betrayed in his pale countenance, the crowd would have demanded again every piece on the programme.

The review served only to irritate. That summer from Nohant Chopin wrote to Fontana about another of Liszt's efforts (12 September):

[His] article on the concert for Cologne Cathedral greatly amused me. And 15,000 persons, counted, *and* the president, *and* the vice-president, *and* the secretary of the Philharmonic Society, *and* that carriage (you know

Liszt - the North Star of empires and horizons, 1841.

what the cabs there are like), *and* that harbour, *and* that steamboat! He will live to be a deputy or perhaps even a king, in Abyssinia or the Congo; but as for the themes of his compositions they will repose in the newspapers...

1841-46 have been called Chopin's 'Years of Asylum' (Mieczysław Tomaszewski). Seventy-two months centered around Sand and the ritual of long summers into autumn in the Loire Valley. Nohant was calm and beautiful. 'Chip-Chip' composed. 'G.S.' – Mme Dudevant, *moja* – wrote. Great minds past through. But it was a place also of tensions, squabbles and ill-humour, of adolescent, irregularly brought-up children, of meddling tongues and people playing off one another. Sunshine-and-meadow hours beatified the days. But then the earth would gasp, and thunder would shake the heavens. Ruffled feathers and flurried tempers would turn into storms and words never taken back. The rebellious Solange wanted to please Chopin, he in turn keeping her amused and giving an occasional lesson. Her mother felt she needed to be cautioned: 'your brother and I love you but we have no illusions about certain faults which you must correct and which you will surely try to eradicate: self-love, a craving to dominate others, and your mad, stupid jealousy'.

Chopin's letters from 1841 say little about his inner demons; and nothing about Maria Wodzińska's marriage to Józef Skarbek, son of his godfather Fryderyk Florian (24 July). But they reveal plenty else. We see him at the piano at creative full-tilt, or at his desk into the late hours – he heads one of his letters '*3 heures du matin. Etoiles*'. We find him working at Cherubini's treatise on counterpoint and fugue (two summers previously having 'corrected' engraving and textual errors in Bach's *Forty Eight*). He's fed up with himself. 'Here the weather has been lovely [...] but my music is hideous' (20 August, four days before finishing the Op. 44 Polonaise). He's frustrated and irritable with his publishers; and even has a go at Fontana, by that autumn a man 'overloaded with instructions and tormented by complexes' (Tomaszewski). Sometimes he's hot-headed, seeing only what he wants to see. 'Wessel [in London] is a rogue; I will never send him anything after *Les Agrémens*... the title he gave my Second Impromptu' (18 September). That *Les Agrémens au Salon* was the auto-suggestive label of a generic collection, under the (comfortable) banner of which the (uncomfortable) Second Sonata had likewise been included, doesn't seem to have occurred to him. The complaining doesn't stop. 'If [Wessel] has made a loss on my compositions, it is doubtless because of those *stupid titles* he gave them, in spite of my forbidding it and in spite of my *repeated railings*' (9 October).

Others nearer home fuelled contemptuous outbursts. Marie de Rozières not least – a bonneted *madame* who made it her business to know, and to pass on, too much about his (Polish) past. Older by five years, she'd had a few free lessons from him in Paris, subsequently supervising some of his 'less talented pupils'. Briefly the mistress of Antoni Wodziński, Maria's brother, as well as Solange's part-time governess, 'she interfered indiscretely in Chopin's private life… and his relations with George Sand and Solange' (Eigeldinger). Outwardly Chopin maintained a degree of civility and professional standing towards her, even dining at her table. 'Blood' friends like Fontana saw another side. 'An insufferable [loose-tongued] pig, who has dug her way in some queer fashion into my private garden, and is rooting |about for truffles among the roses. She is a person to keep away from. Whatever she touches feels her monstrous indiscretion' (24 August). 'The old [sly] frump!… this broomstick… forcing herself into the *intimité* of Mme. S… such a cunning intriguer' (13 September).

Noting his 'exasperating nature', Sand registered his moodiness, informing de Rozières, 20 June:

> A certain person here is irritated with you for reasons I do not know… He is full of spite… He [says] I am… causing trouble between him and his best friends, that my gossiping with you was the cause of it all… The day before yesterday he spent the whole day without speaking a word to anyone. Was he ill? Has somebody annoyed him? Have I said something to upset him? I shall never know… I must not let him think he is the master here—he would be all the more touchy in future… he doesn't know what he wants or does not want.

'Chopin… vents his anger on the piano. When his palfrey fails to obey his commands, he deals him a mighty blow with his fist, such that the poor instrument groans!' (1 August: a specially requested Pleyel, 'almost in chamber-concert tune' but in Chopin's estimation 'very bad', arrived from Paris on the 9th).

Constants and transients dictated life at Nohant. On the one hand, Sand the maternal figure, controlling mistress of the house… 'long-nosed' Chopin comfortably provisioned by the accoutrements of dandyism (preferring Strasbourg *pâté* to coarse dining, he was never naturally a man of the countryside)… her children… her boorish, eternally drunk elder half-brother, Hippolyte Châtiron… peasants and tenants…

On the other, house guests passing time, varying and enlivening the scenery. In 1841 (18 June-4 November) the only visitors of note, in early August, were the twenty-year-old Pauline Viardot and her husband Louis, Director of the Théâtre-Italien. A protégé of Sand's, formerly a student of Liszt and Reicha, and the mezzo in the Mozart *Requiem* for Napoléon, Pauline seems generally to have beguiled – even if Chopin says that 'less time [was spent] on music than on other things' (20 August): going on woodland walks and playing billiards, for instance.

Two reviews that autumn, published within days of each other, kept Chopin, always good 'copy', before the public. In London the Op. 41 Mazurkas sent J. W. Davison into paroxyms (*Musical World*, 28 October):

M[onsieur] Chopin is by no means a putter-down of commonplaces; but he is, what by many would be esteemed worse, a dealer in the most absurd and hyperbolical extravagances… the works of this author invariably give us the idea of an enthusiastic schoolboy whose parts are by no means on a par with his enthusiasm, who *will* be original, whether he *can* or not. There is a clumsiness about his harmonies in the midst of their affected strangeness, a sickliness about his melodies… an utter ignorance of design… the entire works of Chopin present a motley surface of ranting hyperbole and excruciating cacophony… There is no excuse at present for Chopin's delinquencies; he is entrammelled in the enthralling bonds of that arch-enchantress Georges [*sic*] Sand, celebrated equally for the number *and excellence* of her romances and her lovers; none the less we wonder how she… can be content to wanton away her dreamlike existence with an artistic nonentity like Chopin. [Those who] admire Chopin, and they are legion, will admire these mazurkas, which are super-eminently Chopinical. That do *not* we.

In Leipzig, Schumann, less profuse than once, pondered the

Op. 37 Nocturnes, Op. 42 Waltz, and Second Ballade (*Neue Zeitschrift für Muzik*, 2 November):

> Chopin may now publish anything without putting his name to it; his works will always be recognised. This remark includes praise and blame; that for his genius, this for his endeavour... But, though ever new and inventive in the outward forms of his compositions, he remains the same within; and we are almost beginning to fear that he will not rise any higher than he has so far risen. And although this is high enough to render his name immortal in the modern history of art, he limits his sphere to the narrow one of pianoforte music, when, with his powers, he might climb to so great an elevation, and from thence exercise an immense influence on the general progress of our art.

The 'Nohant' Prelude in C sharp minor, Op. 45, 'vast and intimate at one and the same time' (*CFEO*), was published in December as part of a 'Beethoven Album', including Mendelssohn's *Variations sérieuses,* issued in aid of a fund to raise a bronze monument in Bonn to the memory of the Grand Mogul who'd died in Vienna in March 1827*. The magnificent Op. 48 Nocturnes were advertised by Breitkopf and Härtel of Leipzig in the same month. (Within the faltering heart of No. 2 did Schumann come to find perhaps an echo of his own *In der Nacht*, published in 1838?) Reviewing them, the *Revue et Gazette Musicale de Paris* opined that 'the physical aspect is here subordinated to the spiritual side, since the music of Monsieur Chopin demands of the performer, if not his soul, at least imagination, and also that naïve finesse in close kindred to the soul' (17 April 1842).

From November 1841 Chopin lived in his own quarters at Sand's address, 16 rue Pigalle – 'we have almost no time to see one another,' maintained George, 'although we live, if not under one roof, through one wall. He gives lessons the whole day, I scrawl over paper the whole night' (28 December). Passivity seems to have replaced passion. For Sand – de Musset's 'most womanly woman' – he was the 'dear boy', she the 'old mother'. If they loved each other it was no longer, or but rarely, as lovers †. The Paris 'seasons' balanced out the Nohant calendar: teaching the wealthy and perfumed, occasionally undertaking prestige, usually private, concerts, seeing works through to publication,

* Unveiled on 12 August 1845 in the presence of a gathering including Friedrich Wilhelm IV of Prussia, Queen Victoria, Prince Albert, Berlioz, Spohr, Meyerbeer, Moscheles, Hallé, Sir George Smart, Jenny Lind and Pauline Viardot – but also the questionable Lola Montez who disgraced herself and embarrassed Liszt, a prime mover in the festivities, by dancing on a table during the official banquet. Schumann's Fantasy Op. 17, dedicated to Liszt, was an independent contribution to this monument.

† Eighteen months on Sand wrote to the actor Pierre-Martinien Tousez (Bocage), a former lover: 'As for the jealousy of a certain young man over a certain older woman, it is calming down – it had to, for lack of sustenance' (20 July 1843). 'For seven years now [since 1841] I have lived the life of a virgin' (to Grzymała, 12 May 1847).

and entertaining in Sand's salon – the galaxy of intimates including d'Agoult, Balzac, Berlioz, Delacroix, Grzymała, Heine, Liszt, Meyerbeer, Mickiewicz, Viardot and Witwicki…

During 1841-42 he played before court at the Tuileries, a 'white tie' occasion acknowledged with a set of Sèvres porcelain (2 December); and appeared at the Salle Pleyel with Franchomme and Viardot, the solos including the Third Ballade (21 February) and his takings exceeding 5,000 francs – 'something utterly exceptional for Paris, which proves how the public longs to hear the most excellent and most splendid of musicians' (Sand).

Encapsulating the evening, Léon Escudier, all of twenty, took on Liszt as a conjurer of scene (*La France Musicale*, 27 February):

> Chopin has given in Pleyel's rooms a charming *soirée*, a fête peopled with adorable smiles, delicate and rosy faces, small, shapely white hands; a splendid *fête* where simplicity was wedded to grace and elegance, and good taste served as a pedestal to wealth. Gilded ribbons, soft blue gauzes, strings of trembling pearls, the freshest roses and mignonettes, in a word, a thousand of the prettiest and gayest hues, mixed and crossed in endless ways on the perfumed heads and shoulders of the most charming women for whom the princely *salons* contend.

In Nohant that summer (7 May-27 September, interrupted only by a trip to Paris at the beginning of August to find a new place to live), the guests included Delacroix (in June), Witwicki and Viardot. Mademoiselle de Rozières was back, too, probing away: 'I walked at length with Chopin, talking of Poland'. Delacroix can only venerate: 'We carry on endless conversations [… Chopin] is the truest artist I have had occasion to meet in my life. One of those rare individuals whom you can worship and admire at the same time'. Pleyel sent a good piano to play. And on 12 September, Solange – who, her mother says, 'eats like a wolf, swears like a *charretier* and lies like a trooper' – celebrated her fourteenth birthday, Viardot and de Rozières in loving attendance.

Using a converted stable for a studio, Delacroix painted a portrait of St. Anne, patron saint of the village, which was hung in the local church. He also left a few impressions of the place – though without mentioning the village dances that used to take place before the *château* until they were stopped in 1844. At these gatherings Chopin heard a variety of local tunes – sung or foot-stamped, one imagines, to pipes (bagged and blown), violin, the *vielle à roue* (six-stringed 'wheel fiddle'/hurdy-gurdy), perhaps an ill-tempered piano or guitar. A couple of *bourrées** scribbled in Sand's music album surfaced subsequently in her play *François le Champi*, produced at the Odéon in Paris in 1849.

In October 1842 Chopin and Sand settled in the artist colony of Square d'Orléans adjoining Montmartre (80 rue Taitbout/34 rue St. Lazaire, *arrondissement* 9) – he at No. 9, at an annul rent of 600 francs, she on the opposite side of the courtyard at No 5. Carlotta Marliani occupied No. 7. 'The Cité d'Orléans was a new district of large proportions, with a spacious court – the first of its kind – and a number of apartments, with numbers, and a name (Cité), is always popular with Parisians. It lay behind the rue de Provence, one of the fashionable quarters… It looked – as indeed it was – aristocratic' (von Lenz). To Károly Filtsch's elder brother, Joseph, we owe a description of Chopin's rooms:

> We crossed a garden and reached the house in which Chopin occupied the first floor [mezzanine] – a small but refined, dainty apartment where everything points to an exceptional taste from the pretty design of the carpets to the handsome embroidered [cushions]; a beautiful "service" of gold (*vermeil*) with the crest of Louis-Philippe, some vases in marble, bronze candelabras, and an old rococo clock on the mantlepiece… [A] beautiful piano stood open… [noiselessly] a man of medium height about 38 or 40 [in fact 31] entered the room. His frail suffering physiognomy was animated by expressive eyes. I was struck by the large arteries on his forehead; his thick, blond hair naturally curled, was brushed back flat against the head; his whole appearance expressed regret, physical suffering and dreaminess… he left the room and shortly returned with a lady… George Sand. Medium size, well made, curls falling over her shoulders, her eyes beautifully shaped… Her black dress, buttoned up to the neck, made her look manly, but there is no truth in the malicious report that she wears men's clothes †.

The major works of 1842, offered to Breitkopf on 15 December, were the Polonaise in A flat, Op. 53, the Fourth

* First published in 1968, edited by the present author (Schott, London). For some of the 'humble wild flowers' of 19th/20th century French village life, *les chants de la terre*, reflecting 'the ambiguities of middle-class interest in folk music', see François Lazarevitch's *La veillée imaginaire* (CD: Alpha 528 [2010]).

† Irene Andrews, *About One Whom Chopin Loved*, 1923; Ferdinand Gajewski, 'New Chopiniana from the papers of Carl Filtsch', *Studi Musicali*, Vol XI/i, 1982, delivered originally at a meeting of the Mid-Atlantic Chapter of the American Musicological Society, 11 October 1980.

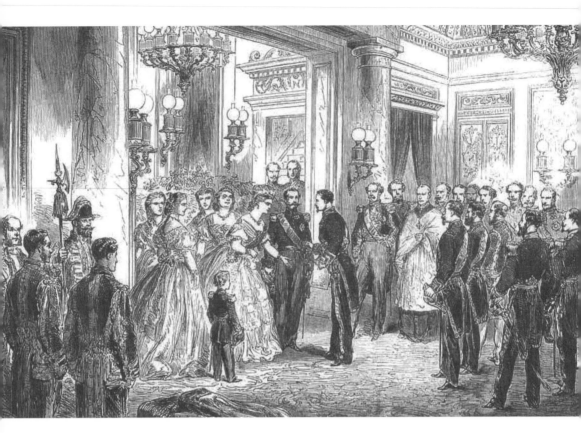

The Château de Saint-Cloud, Napoléon's preferred residence.

Ballade, and the Fourth Scherzo. Of these the Polonaise (dedicated to the Paris-based German Jewish banker Auguste Leo, a relative of Moscheles), together with the later Polonaise-Fantaisie, culminated Chopin's development of the genre. Gutmann relates how 'Chopin could thunder forth in the way we are accustomed to hear it. As for the famous octave passages which occur in it, he began them *pianissimo* and continued them without much increase in loudness… Chopin never thumped.' Hallé reminds that he was no speed merchant either: '[Once] in his gentle way he laid his hand upon my shoulder, saying how unhappy he felt because he had heard his *Grande Polonaise* in A flat, *jouée vite*! – thereby destroying all the grandeur, the majesty of this noble inspiration. Poor Chopin must be rolling round and round in his grave nowadays, for this misreading has unfortunately become the fashion' (*Autobiography*). Among 'occasional pieces' was the G flat Impromptu, Op. 51, finished in the autumn. Two versions of this exist – the earlier *without* the later's double-notes. Research in the 1980s wondered if the revision migh have been prompted by Károly Filtsch, Chopin's twelve-year-old Transylvanian protégé – who sometime in late 1842 or early 1843 had shown his teacher an impromptu he'd written in the same key and time-signature *with* double-notes. Chopin adored him: 'Nobody has ever understood me like this child does… It is not imitation, it is the same sentiment, an instinct that makes him play without thinking, as if it could not have been any other way' (*Der Humorist*, Vienna, February 1843). Filtsch died of tuberculosis in Venice in 1845, seventeen days shy of his fifteenth birthday.

Following a concert in Janury at the Rothschilds (Károly playing the E minor Concerto, to the composer's 'orchestral' piano accompaniment)… Liszt in Warsaw paying his respects to Chopin's parents and Elsner (April) – Nicholas taking the view that 'you do well not to split with him… you have been good friends'… and Balzac's iconic pronouncement, 'You cannot judge Liszt without having heard Chopin. The Hungarian is a demon, the Pole is an angel' (May)… everyone was back in Nohant for the summer of '43 (22 May-28 October, Sand staying on into November), some taking the new train-line to Blois. Pauline Viardot came with her new little daughter, Louisette, doted upon by everybody.

Summers at Nohant emphasised-contrived conviviality. But the pleasure Chopin took from his friends, his amateur dramatics, his donkey riding, the satisfaction Sand got from her domestic routine and 'traditional' jam-making, her 'writing, painting and having a good time,' came at escalating personal cost. Chopin liked the place yet at the same time resisted it. Rurality was not his natural habitat. Sand, nearing forty, would find her energy and spirit ebbing away. 'The sad state of health of our friend has lent our lifestyle a melancholy or perhaps a reflectiveness' (7 May 1843). 'The house is lacking in joy, and I feel very lonely, though the good Chopin talks to me constantly… and does everything to amuse both himself and me… swallows are nesting above the dining-room windows… it is quiet here and no-one frightens them away' (13 June). 'I am utterly weary and feel the need to return to a peaceful family life' (early August). To Delacroix: 'Were it possible, I would say: come and spend the last days of autumn with me. But Your life is tied [up], just like mine. If You were in my hands, I would tend to You *comme il faut*, and You would be as strong as an ox. You might listen to me better than Chopin' (4 November). Twelve days later she writes to Maurice, touching on Chopin's condition (he was back under medical attention): 'His letters are sad and brief. Take care of him… Stand in for me a little'. His 'lamentable' health (he is 'little to be seen,'

Heine reports) persisted throughout the winter and spring (Paris being in the grip of an influenza epidemic in February). In June he is 'horribly tormented by toothache'. His Polish student, Zofia Rosengardt, who studied with him between November 1843 and March 1844, noted all the signs of frustration and unpredictability betraying a body in discord. 'He has... some wild, painful, nasty and angry moments when he breaks chairs and stamps his feet. He is as capricious as a spoilt child, scolds his pupils, treats his friends coldly. This happens mostly on days when he's ill, physically weak, or has argued with Madame Sand'.

1844, Friday May 3rd. In Warsaw Chopin's father dies – from 'age and exhaustion following a life of hard work... his gaze wandered to your portrait and bust, he gave up his soul to God' (Antoni Barcínski, Chopin's brother-in-law through his sister Izabela). 'He is distraught... he wants to see no-one,' Sand says, telling his mother: 'You know the depth of his pain, but thank God he is not ill. I devote my days to Your son; I consider him as my own son' *.

> The Catholic dogma throws on death horrible terrors. Chopin, instead of dreaming [of a better world for his father's soul], had only dreadful visions, and I was obliged to pass very many nights in a room adjoining his, always ready to rise a hundred times from my work in order to drive away the spectres of his sleep and wakefulness. The idea of his own death appeared to him accompanied with all the superstitious imaginings of Slavonic poetry. As a Pole he lived under the nightmare of legends. The phantoms called him, clasped him, and, instead of seeing his father and his friend smile at him in the ray of faith, he repelled their fleshless faces from his own and struggled under the grasp of their icy hands [*Histoire de ma vie*].

* Accounts differ as to when Chopin received the news. Tomaszewski (Fryderyk Chopin Institute) suggests as late as May 25th, Sand apparently telling Chopin following a performance at the Odéon of *Antigone* at which they'd been joined by Lamartine and Hugo. Hedley (1962) claimed around the 10th, assigning to the 12th an undated letter from Sand advising Franchomme of Chopin's grief (formerly attributed to the 26th by Sydow).

That year six months were spent at Nohant (29 May-28 November), with interim trips to Paris. Two masterworks at opposite ends of the spectrum resulted. The Berceuse, Op. 57 – 'who will cut open the nightingale's throat to discover where the song comes from?' (Hedley). And the Third Sonata, in B minor, Op. 58 – where Chopin surpassed himself. Liszt copied it out, varying the finale. Brahms edited it. And Franz Brendel (not known for being a Chopin worshipper) hailed it as 'one of the

Chopin: oil portrait by Teofil Kwiatkowski, *c.* 1843, attributed formerly to Luigi Rubio.

most significant publications of the present'. Its four movements – spanning worlds of experience vast in depth, eloquent in breadth, bejewelled in song – embrace the proud, the mercurial, the hallowed, the volcanic. Their passage, from declamation to affirmation, Romantic enchantment to that last 'ride of an imaginary horseman, of a dream Mazeppa, galloping towards the horizon' fancied by Cortot, is one for all time.

Between 13 July and 3 September Chopin's sister Ludwika and her husband, Józef Kalasanty Jędrzejewicz (a professor of law), came to visit and comfort. Chopin showed them Paris, where they stayed in Sand's apartment, before bringing them to Nohant: 'I would only urge you.' Sand writes in advance (in a letter stressing the propriety of their relationship), 'to see that little Chopin – for that is what we call your brother, the great Chopin – has a good rest before he is allowed to set off for our Berry province. It is a journey of eighty leagues and is rather tiring for him'. 'You will find our [my] dear boy very frail and greatly altered since you last saw him! But do not be alarmed about his health. It has remained pretty much the same during the last six years when I have seen him every day… The joy of seeing you, although mingled with deep and painful emotions,

Chopin in Nohant: pencil drawing by Sand, summer 1844. Given by Sand to Ludwika. Lost in Warsaw in 1939. 'The deepest, fullest vehicle of emotions and feelings ever to have existed. He has made a single instrument speak the language of infinity'- George Sand

will shatter his spirit somewhat on the first day, but it will do him much good...'

Ludwika and Józef stayed at Nohant for nearly three weeks (August 9-28), integrating themselves in the household, getting to know Sand, and enjoying Solange's pretty company. Chopin saw them back to Paris, giving a musical *soirée* before their return home. '3 September, half past two after midnight' written in Polish on an album leaf of (Witwicki's) *Wiosna* suggests the evening lasted well into the small hours.

Chopin, refreshed by reunion and mother-tongue, wrote to Ludwika a fortnight later : 'Often, when I come in, I look to see if there is nothing left of you, and I see only the place by the couch, where we drank our chocolate... More of you has remained in my room; on the table lies your embroidery – that slipper, wrapped in tissue-paper – folded inside an English blotter, and on the piano a tiny pencil, which was in your pocketbook, and which I find most useful... Your old Ch.' (18 September).

On the last day of October Chopin sends her another letter, picturing life in Nohant but also hinting at irritation with Maurice, now become a swaggering, smoking, sniggering twenty-one-year-old, with a touch of cruelty compounded by lack of gallantry:

> I expect to stay here two or three more weeks. The leaves have not all fallen, only turned yellow, and the weather has been fine for a week; the Lady of the House profits by this for various planting and arranging of that courtyard in which, you remember, they danced. There is to be a big lawn and flowerbeds. The idea is to put, opposite the dining room door, a door leading from the billiard room to the greenhouse (what we call an orangery)... Sol[ange] is not very well today; she is sitting in my room and asks me to send you hearty greetings. Her brother (courtesy is not in his nature, so don't be surprised that he has given me no message for your husband about that little machine for cigars) is leaving here next month to go to his father for a few weeks, and will take his uncle Hippolyte with him, so as not to be bored.

In December, while Sand is still at Nohant, he buys her some dress fabric, 'from the black Levant, of the best quality; very beautiful, modest, but in good taste'; and pictures her 'in the morning, in Your dressing-gown, surrounded by Your dear children'. Compatibly disposed, they go to the theatre in the New Year; and in March attend performances at the Conservatoire of Mozart's *Requiem* and Haydn's *Creation*. At the end of May they encounter some painted 'savages', a troupe of Iowa Indians brought over from the borderlands of Nebraska and Northeast Kansas by the New World artist-showman George Catlin – the topic of Sand's article *Une visite chez les sauvages de Paris.*

'Love begins with fine feelings,' says Maurois, 'and ends in trivial quarrels… the atmosphere at Nohant *seemed* to be one of gaiety, poetry and genius… but peace of mind was absent'. Preceded by a snow-flurried Paris spring, the 1845 Nohant season (13 June-28 November, floods and storms at first, then hot and balmy, followed by an 'abundant' harvest) saw tensions flaring into the open. Maurice wanted to reject Chopin's friendship, resenting his presence and the hold he had over his mother. (In later years, endeavouring to distort the facts and nature of their union, he suppressed a number of passages in their correspondence.) Solange, on the other hand – on the cusp of seventeen, 'big, beautiful' and flirtatious – liked to take Chopin on distracting rides in the cabriolet and enjoyed duets and chess with him. The addition of a distant cousin to the *ménage* – Augustine Brault ('beauty and goodness incarnate') whom Sand adopted officially the following spring – complicated the dynamic. To Maurice she was an object of (disposable) infatuation; to Solange a girl to be trifled with and humiliated. In the conflicts to unfold, Maurice and Augustine set themselves against Chopin and Solange, with Sand swaying rockily in between, initially neutral but then progressively taken in by her son.

Chopin's servant, Jan, the only person with whom he could speak Polish, was an early victim of the pernicious climate. Maurice disliked him. Sand's maid, Suzanne, complained about him. 'The two are often at loggerheads, and since [she] is very clever, quick and indispensable it may be that I shall have to get rid of my man for the sake of the peace' (16-20 July). By the time Chopin returned to Paris for the winter (28 November), Jan was gone. 'I would never have dismissed him but he exasperated the others – the children made fun of him too much' (12-26 December).

On lighter days Chopin kept the family in Warsaw abreast of trivialities – dancing on the cut grass before the church;

bagpipes and terpsichore at the local fair at Sarzay; the *château* dogs. Of gossip – in Paris Victor Hugo, in his forties, gets caught with someone else's wife and is 'suddenly' away on his travels: Juliette Drouet, the actress and former courtesan, 'whom Hugo has long kept as his woman, in spite of Mme. Hugo, his children and his poems on family morality' goes off with him. Of the world at large – 'the electric telegraph between Baltimore and Washington is giving wonderful [speedy] results'. Of the incredulous – 'In Bonn [celebrating the new Beethoven monument] they are selling "genuine Beethoven cigars" – Beethoven, who certainly smoked nothing but Viennese pipes; and they have already sold so much old furniture, old desks and bookcases "belonging to Beethoven" that the poor composer of the *Pastoral Symphony* must have had a vast furniture business'.

Letter writing aside, Chopin's creativity was at a standstill. Even the piano was silent: 'I play little, the [instrument] is out of tune'. 'Oh, how time flies. I don't know how it is, but I can't do anything decent... I spend whole days and evenings in my own room. But I simply must finish certain manuscripts before I leave here, for I cannot compose in winter' (1-5 August). It wasn't until the autumn that he started three important new works – the Barcarolle, Polonaise-Fantaisie, and Cello Sonata, written for Franchomme.

The winter of 1845 and spring of 1846 see the dried-up lovers maladious but in relative harmony. On November 29th, returning to Paris via her cousins at Chenonceau (near Tours), Sand writes: 'Nohant. Saturday evening. Midnight... In Paris you must allow yourself time for three good nights, and don't over-tire yourself. Love me, my dear angel, my dear joy. I love you'. They go to the theatre, opera and ballet. And in January and February attend charity balls at the 17th century Hôtel Lambert on the Île Saint-Louis, owned by Prince Adam Jerzy Czartoryski, noblest Polish political voice of the age. At the end of April Chopin – according to Sand 'more quarrelsome and picking holes than usual: I find it funny, Mademoiselle de Rozières is driven to tears, Solange pays it back with interest' – gives a party, 'with music, flowers and a grand spread'. The Czartoryskis, Delacroix and Viardot come. Louis Blanc – the utopian socialist who in 1839 famously pronounced 'from each according to his abilities, to each according to his needs' – makes 'superb proposals to Titine [Augustine]'. A month later – and another Nohant summer (27 May-12 November). Delacroix, Grzymała, Viardot, the young Matthew Arnold from Oxford

- who, over midday breakfast, admires Chopin's 'wonderful eyes' but finds the lady of the house a creature of no more than 'frank, cordial simplicity', unastonishing in appearance (1877).

Soirées to midnight – 'from buoyant moods to sadness, from mirth to solemnity… Wonderful simplicity, sweetness, goodness and wit' (Élise Fournier, 9 July). Improvisations, songs, 'divine' Beethoven. Sporadic composition – 'Dear friend, I am doing my best to work but I am stuck and if it goes on like that, my new productions [Barcarolle, Polonaise-Fantaisie, Nocturnes Op. 62] will neither give the impression of warbling birds nor even of broken china. I must accept my lot' (to Franchomme, 8 July).

Among Sand's publications in 1846 was the pastoral novel *La Mare au Diable* (written in four days the previous autumn), inscribed 'à mon ami F. Chopin' (not that he ever dedicated anything to her). And, from 25 June, the serialisation in *Courier Français* of *Lucrezia Floriani*, which Sand would read to guests around the fireside. What they heard confirmed rumours that here was a thinly disguised account of her affair with Chopin. She denied any resemblance. Whatever the vogue (she lied), real people, the loves and hates of one's life, were not for putting into novels. The main protagonists are Prince Karol, an artist, delicate and refined, whose jealousies, beliefs and negativity finally cause him to kill his mistress, Lucrezia Floriani, an actress no longer young or beautiful. Any similarity between Chopin and Sand might have ended there, but she went further. Karol is six years younger than Lucrezia; he has Mallorcan hallucinations; 'the more [his] irritability increased, the more polite and reserved did he appear: his icy courtesy was the measure of his fury… he became mannered. He affected to view everything and everybody with disgust… When he lacked the courage to contradict and jeer, he took refuge in disdainful silences and fits of heartbreaking sulkiness'. Lucrezia is presented as an experienced woman with a string of past lovers; she cares little for Karol's religious scruples and encourages social freedom; her son is a replica of Maurice… Passages from *Lucrezia Floriani* were later quoted almost *verbatim* in Sand's autobiography – the portraits of Prince Karol in the one and Chopin in the other are interchangeable. Liszt, acceptingly, drew on the novel for 'facts' in his biography of Chopin.

Friends were dismayed. 'I was in agony while she was reading. The executioner and the victim surprised me equally. Madame Sand appeared to be completely at her ease, and

Chopin was in raptures over the story' (Delacroix). 'How terribly *Lucrezia* disgusted me!... Madame Sand, in the general holocaust of pianists, gives us Chopin on a platter with all the distasteful domestic details, in cold blood, which nothing can excuse. It is as though some second self had taken control of her. Women can never be too much on their guard against these betrayals of the bed-chamber... Why does so fine a genius allow herself to be so ill inspired?' (Hortense Allart). 'That advocate of women's rights treated my friend Chopin insultingly in a hideous novel, divinely written' (Heine). Whether Chopin recognised himself in Karol isn't known; certainly he gave no immediate sign of being offended: 'the truth was,' according to Delacroix, 'that he just had not understood'. To his family he merely observed that it 'has aroused less enthusiasm... than [Sand's] other books' (19 April 1847).

That hot summer of 1846 – 'more lovely than they remember here for a long time' – was to be Chopin's last at Nohant. It 'hasn't been bad for me,' Sand reported, 'even if he constantly moans, and... suffers from an eternal, indefinable ill disposition. But he eats and sleeps [perspires and 'stinks'] like anyone else and hasn't lain in bed for a single day since we got here' (to Marie de Rozières, 18 June; Carlotta Marliani, 3 October). Taking 'courage' from his 'sweetness' to tell him 'a few home truths,' she noted on 8 August, she 'threatened him with the possibility that [her] patience might not last... he has since been in a more reasonable frame of mind, and you know how good, admirable, and excellent he can be when he is not mad'.

On 11 October Chopin wrote another of his 'Polish' family letters, beginning 'my dearest ones... [sitting] at the table by the piano'. The letter suggests a conscious attempt to avoid the bigger issues of the moment. There was much comment on the pastoral niceties of life at Nohant, a surfeit of small-talk, and some enthusiastic comment on the recent discovery of the planet Neptune. But despite the effort there persist one or two paragraphs which are edgy in tone, voicing something perhaps of Chopin's truer frame of mind:

> The whole summer has been spent here on various drives and excursions in the unknown district of the Vallée Noire. I was not *de la partie*, for these things tire me more than they are worth. I am so weary, so depressed, that it reacts on the mood of the others, and the young folk enjoy things better without me... I should like to fill my letter

with good news, but I know none, except that I love you and love you. I play a little, I write a little [the summer mainly saw the completion of the Barcarolle, Polonaise-Fantaisie and Cello Sonata]. Sometimes I am satisfied with my violoncello Sonata, sometimes not. I throw it into the corner, then take it up again… When one does a thing, it appears good, otherwise one would not write it. Only later comes reflection, and one discards or accepts the thing. Time is the best censor and patience a most excellent teacher.

The same day Sand dropped a few lines to Delacroix: 'Stripped of my torments and my inner storms, I'm not bored by anything, and I'm delighted by everything at hand. And you too, dear artist, you're delighted by a dog, a fly, a blade of grass… Chopin interrupts me to tell me he adores you' (11 October).

He – short on love – returned to a 'dark and damp' Paris in mid-November; Sand – 'love and I having long since gone our separate ways' (9 December) – followed in February 1847, attending a chamber music *soirée* on the 21st with Chopin and Delacroix.

In the autumn of 1846, with Chopin's approval, the eighteen-year-old Solange announced her engagement to Fernand de Préaulx, a young *vicomte* of breeding if not much intelligence. 'He certainly will not set the Seine on fire,' rued Sand. 'He knows nothing of our modern civilisation, [having] spent his life in the backwoods with horses, wild boars and wolves…' Within months, however, a new distraction had appeared on the horizon: one Auguste Jean Baptiste Clésinger – a bearded, 'noisy, disorderly creature, a former cavalry soldier turned sculptor, who [carries] with him… the manners of the canteen and the studio' (Arséne Houssaye). Loud, boorish and persistent, headstrong as a stallion, 'all fire and flame', Clésinger had designs on Solange, who, succumbing, jilted Préaulx at the last moment (26 February). A scandal erupted and in early April – Delacroix meanwhile having shown Chopin and Sand their likenesses, as Dante and Aspasia, on the dome of the Palais de Luxembourg – the family retreated to Nohant, pursued by Clésinger, 'violently in love'. He proposed to Solange on the 13th, and on 19 May 1847 the couple were hastily married.

Sand informed Chopin late, by letter: 'it doesn't concern him, and when once the Rubicon has been crossed the "ifs" and "buts" only do harm,' she wrote to Maurice (16 April).

Solange Dudevant-Sand (1828-99):
bust by Auguste Clésinger.

Too unwell to get involved, Chopin's reaction to his favourite marrying such a 'stupid, brutal' drunkard and debtor as Clésinger, an older man of 'shady affairs... [without] friends or connections', was low-key. To the girl herself: 'You are at the summit of bliss – and that is how I should like to see You always. From the bottom of my heart I wish You unchanging prosperity'. To his family (8 June): 'Sol's marriage took place in the village during my illness – to be honest, I am not vexed about it, as I do not know what sort of face I could have put on... It was a moment of madness which did not last a month – and there was no one there to pour cold water on it all... The marriage has... made a bad impression in Parisian society, for one of [Clésinger's recent] statues... represents a woman in a most indecent pose*... The way she writhes is frightful... I may say between ourselves that all Madame Sand's real old friends cannot get over this extraordinary marriage – not one of them was at the wedding.'

'If Chopin can be moved,' Sand advised Grzymała, 12 May, 'I shall bring him back [to Nohant] with me':

> I think he has suffered a good deal in his solitude from knowing nothing and being unable to give any advice. But it is no good paying attention to anything he says when the problem to be solved has to do with real life. He has never been able to face facts, not can he even begin to understand human nature. His being is all poetry and music, and he cannot bear what is different from himself... It is all very difficult and very delicate. I can think of no way of calming and restoring a sick mind, when every effort to effect a cure merely irritates the invalid. The evil which is eating away the poor creature, both morally and physically, has been for me, over a long period of time, a form of slow death. I see him slipping away without being able to do a thing to help him, because it is the very uneasiness, jealousy and moodiness of his affection for me that is the chief cause of his melancholy.

Viewing her as 'an adorable *maman* [without] a pennyworth of practical common sense' - 'she sometimes does not speak the truth' - Chopin stayed on in Paris.

In June, cousin 'Titine' became engaged to a friend of Maurice's, Théodore Rousseau, a bourgeois Parisian painter admired for his naturescapes. Sand encouraged the romance,

* *Woman bitten by a serpent* (marble, Musée d'Orsay)

promising a generous dowry. Never Augustine's ally, Solange – 'strong-minded, tenacious, cold, cynical, remorseless and pitiless' – was having none of it. She let loose a whirlwind of calamity, accusation and malicious gossip, described by Sand in a letter to the Provençal poet Charles Poncy, 27 August:

> No sooner married than she has trampled everything under foot, and dropped the mask. She has turned her hot-blooded but weak-minded husband against me, against Maurice, and against Augustine, for whom she entertains a mortal hatred, and whose only fault lies in being far too good and far too devoted. It is entirely owing to her that the poor child's [intended] marriage has broken down, and that Rousseau has gone temporarily insane. She repeated to him the most atrocious lies about Maurice and Augustine [that they had been lovers]… she is doing her best to embroil me with my friends… she poses as the victim of my unjust preference for her brother… She has fouled the nest in which she was reared by thinking – and saying – that it has been the scene of the most disgraceful conduct.

The feud grew ugly, 'scarcely to be believed'. 'We have been within an ace of cutting one another's throat'. At one point Clésinger takes a hammer to Maurice – who would have shot him but for the intervention of G.S. She punches Clésinger, only to be punched back in the chest (striking women wasn't new for him: he'd done it before to a pregnant mistress). 'And there stood Solange,' she records, 'stirring the flames with icy ferocity.' Thrown out of Nohant, 'the devilish couple took themselves off yesterday evening [11 July], crippled with debts, glorying in their impudence, and leaving behind them a scandal the effects of which they will never be able to shake off. Here I was, for three days, in my own house, at the mercy of a murderer. I never want to see them again. They shall never cross my threshold. This is the last straw! Dear God, what have I done to deserve such a daughter!' (to Marie de Rozières). Ruthlessly excised, Solange's presence at Nohant was to be no more, her boudoir turned into a theatre space within months.

Blaming the breakdown on her mother rather than husband, Solange, by now in the nauseous stages of early pregnancy, wrote to Chopin from La Châtre, a short distance south of Nohant, asking for his carriage to get back to Paris, Sand and

Maurice having 'positively refused' to let her have it ('Sunday evening', 11 July). Chopin, unsuspecting of the arena he was about to enter, obliged: 'I am much grieved to know that you are unwell. I hasten to place my carriage at your service. I have written to this effect to your mother. Look after yourself' ('Wednesday', 14 July)*. Chopin had always had a soft spot for Solange, and it was not going to change. 'For many years he was captivated by her charms… His feelings for her were profound, initially fatherly, [then more complex]… as the child becomes a girl, and the girl a woman' (the politician Emmanuel Arago, one of Sand's republican friends). The immediate correspondence between Chopin and Sand is lost, or was destroyed. But evidently Chopin's instruction was seen as 'a slap in the face' (Hedley), his taking of sides an act of 'betrayal' and 'disloyalty' (Samson). Never one to hold back, she fired off a letter. Chopin read it to Delacroix – who wrote in his journal: '… an atrocious letter. Bitter passions and long-suppressed impatience are plainly discernible, with a contrast that would be almost funny if the whole affair were not so sad; from time to time she plays the woman's part and bursts into tirades which might have been taken straight from a novel, or a sermon on philosophy' (20 July). Resorting impersonally to *vous*, Chopin replied on the 24th: 'As for [Solange] – I cannot remain indifferent… Ill fortune may cast a shadow over [your children], but cannot alter their nature. This misfortune must be very powerful today if it can forbid your heart to listen to any mention of your daughter, at the beginning of her real life as a woman, at the very moment when her physical condition calls more than ever for a mother's care'.

Next day, Sunday, Sand wrote to de Rozières:

> At long last I received a letter by this morning's post from Chopin!… all this time, while I have been spending sleepless nights worrying over the state of his health, he has been thinking ill of me and condoling with the Clésinger couple. A fine state of affairs, I must say! The solemnity with which he writes makes me laugh! He preaches to me for all the world like a good father and family man… There is a lot behind this at which I can only guess, but I do know of just how much credulity and prejudice my daughter is capable.

She replied to Chopin on the 28th, her last (known) letter to him:

* Solange's request and Chopin's reply, both undated, are customarily attributed a week later to 18 and 21 July respectively – which does not agree with the chronology of events so far as can be established.

Very well, my friend, follow now the dictates of your heart and assume that it is the voice of your conscience. I understand perfectly… It would ill become [Solange] to say that she needs her mother's love – a mother whom she hates and slanders, whose most innocent actions and whose home she blackens by the most frightful calumnies. You choose to listen to it all and maybe believe what she says. I do not propose to wage a war of that kind. I prefer to see you pass over to the enemy rather than defend myself from a foe bred of my flesh and reared on my milk. Look after her then, since it is she to whom you think you must devote yourself. I shall not hold it against you, but you will understand that I am going to maintain my right to play the part of the outraged mother, and henceforth nothing will induce me to allow the authority and dignity of my role to be slighted. I have had enough of being a dupe and a victim. I forgive you, and from now on I shall not utter one word of reproach, for you have made a sincere confession. It surprises me somewhat, but if, having made it, you feel freer and easier in your mind, I shall not suffer from this strange *volte face*. *Adieu, mon ami…* I shall thank God for this *bizarre dénouement* to nine years of exclusive friendship. Let me hear now and then how you are. There is no point in ever discussing the other matters.

To her friends she expressed relief. To Arago, 26 July:

Chopin, who was to come [to Nohant] and suddenly does not… has become completely different in his attitude towards me, he no longer dies from mortal love, which I could not requite, as his friends accused me, and he declares to me that I am a bad mother… What burdensome ties have been broken… his narrow-minded and despotic way of thinking… In all my life I have never seen anything as offensive as his absurd jealousy… Thank God that it is not I who will kill him, and I can finally begin a new life.

To Carlotta Marliani, 2 November:

Chopin has openly sided with [Solange] against me, and that without knowing the truth, which smacks of

Chopin by August Weger. This engraving was based on a less flattering portrait by Ary Scheffer sketched in Nohant in 1846 and finished in Paris in 1847. Daguerreotyped in 1862, Scheffer's original, together with Izabela's collection of her brother's letters and effects inherited from their mother, was lost on 19 September 1863 when Russian soldiers ransacked and burnt the Warsaw palace of Count Andrzej Zamoyski – leading to the Count's exile in France, the defenestration of one of Chopin's instruments, and the writing of Cyprian Norwid's iconic free-verse poem, *Chopin's Piano*.

ingratitude to me and of crazy infatuation for her... He has changed so much that I can only assume that she has worked upon his jealous and suspicious nature, and that it is by her and her husband that this absurd slander has been put about touching a *love affair* on my part, or an exclusive friendship, in connection with the young man you mention [Victor Borie, an aspiring journalist and house guest that summer – to whose *Travailleurs et propriétaires* Sand contributed an introduction two years later]... I am far from feeling annoyed that [Chopin] should have decided to take the management of his life out of my hands. Both he and his friends were beginning to put a great deal too much responsibility on my shoulders... from the evidence of his own eyes [Maurice knew] how chaste our relationship was, but could not help seeing, too, how the poor sickly creature, without wishing to, and perhaps because he could not help it, behaved as though he were my lover, my husband, and the master of my every thought and action... He had a horror, and a furious, insanable jealousy, of everyone – men and women alike, and no matter what their age... I could stand it no longer. His own particular circle will, I know, take a very different view. He will be looked upon as a victim, and the general opinion will find it pleasanter to believe that I, in spite of my age [43], have got rid of him in order to take another lover...

On 18 November Chopin's Pleyel grand was returned to Paris, rebuffing a message from Solange that her mother could keep it at Nohant: 'I have no wish that Chopin should make me a present of a piano. I do not like being under an obligation to those who hate me. What Chopin has said to his friends in confidence – and like all confidences, it has been passed on – make it quite clear how he and I stand...' (to de Rozières, 22 November). 'A strange creature, with all her intellect ! Some kind of frenzy has come upon her ; she harrows up her own life, she harrows up her daughter's life; with her son too it will end badly... I do not regret that I helped her through the eight most difficult years of her [motherhood]... I do not regret what I have suffered; but I am sorry that the daughter, that carefully over-cultivated plant, sheltered from so many storms, has been broken in her mother's hand by a carelessness and levity pardonable perhaps in a woman in her twenties, but not in one in her forties'

Chopin's apartment at Square
d'Orléans 9, his Pleyel by the window.
Unsigned watercolour.

(Chopin to Ludwika and the family, Christmas 1847 [6 January
1848]).

A couple of months later, near enough a year since they'd last
met, the two bumped into each other at Madame Marliani's new
place. 4 March 1848. Saturday. He tells her that Solange has just
had a little girl, Jeanne Gabrielle – who lives for no more than
a week. Bowing, he goes downstairs. 'I took his hand. It was icy
cold and trembling. I should have liked to talk with him, but he
took to his heels… I never saw him again.'

'That is the way of the world,' Maurois reflects. 'Two people
may be all in all to one another, but habit plays a large part in
their daily intimacy. Transplant them, separate them, and very
soon they will strike new roots in strange soil. To the friend
whom once we made the confidant of our every thought, we
cannot bring ourselves to say a word. Silence covers all. The
heart bleeds for Sand and Chopin meeting for a moment on the
staircase of that house in the rue de la Ville-l'Évêque [No. 18],
going their ways, and never, for a moment, looking back.'

Chopin, the 'Shakespeare, Byron
and Mickiewicz of pianists' - Antoni
Woykowski. Sand's 'evil genius, her
moral vampire, her cross' - Mickiewicz.

Chopin photographed by Louis-
Auguste Bisson, late 1847. 40 kilos,
'whiskerless, beardless, fair of hair'.
Bisson took this early photograph,
formerly ascribed to 1849, at his
Paris *atelier*, 65, rue Saint-Germain-
l'Auxerrois.

II. Albion

Above: Auguste Franchomme (1808–84): portrait by Jean-Auguste-Alfred Masson. 'Perform Chopin's works with the same accuracy as you do the works of the old masters. Bear in mind that a note repeated from the arm, a third beat unduly accented, a note lifted too hastily all suffice to distort the poetry of the composer's work and place you in the category of his *massacreurs*'.

In February 1847 Chopin completed the Cello Sonata which on 23 March he ran through privately with Franchomme at a musical evening in his rooms honouring the birthday of his 'ravishingly beautiful' former student Countess Delfina Potocka, the 'muse of Polish Romanticism' ('who you know how I love'), dedicatee of the F minor Concerto and D flat Waltz. Op. 64 No. 1. Anna and Adam Czartoryski and Sand attended. Fancifully as much inner lament as wider prophecy, its ghost-trails journey demonstrably between an unfinished Mallorcan Canon (the finale) and Schubert's *Der Winterreise – Gute Nacht* in particular*: 'The lover has come to realize the worthlessness of his beloved and knows at last that the love, which was the greatest experience of his life, has been squandered on one who was incapable of appreciating the unique gift of true love and faith. The girl had playfully accepted her lover's pledge and then without any compunction had broken his heart. He struggles to escape from his devotion to her. He tries to leave the surroundings where he has been so deeply wounded and betrayed' (Lotte Lehmann).

Between 1838 and 1846 Delfina's lover had been one of Mickiewicz's friends, Count Zygmunt Krasiński, a Parisian-born patriot, philospher and poet – 'representative of the noblest trends of the thought of his time, and eloquently expressive of his nation's sufferings… one of the mightiest minds that Poland ever brought forth' (Stanislaus Tarnowski). Sometime in 1847 Chopin wrote one last song *(Melodya* [*Onward* in the original English edition] Op. 74 No. 9), setting lines by Krasiński, *Z gór, gdzie dźwigali strasznych krzyżów brzemię* – music of high art and perfect finish moving expressively from *maggiore* warmth to *minore* melancholy.

The poet says:

From the hills, where they carried the load of nightmarish

* The Schubertian dimension/ derivation of the first movement – Chopin turning to *Winterreise* 'at the time of his highly painful separation from George Sand' – is examined by Anatole Leiken in *The Cambridge Companion to Chopin* (1992).

crosses, they saw from a distance the promised land. They saw light's heavenly rays, towards which in the valley their tribe was dragging its load, some of them will not enter those infinite spaces! the comforts of life they will never sit down, and even, perhaps, they will be forgotten *.

In Delfina's copy Chopin added the 'Nella miseria' from Dante's *Inferno*: 'There is no greater sorrow than to recall a time of happiness in misery.'

1848 opened with a royal funeral – Louis-Philippe's sister and confidante, Adélaïde, had died on New Year's Eve. And a concert in Pleyel's salon on Wednesday16 February – Chopin's last Paris appearance as a pianist. 'All the seats were sold out a week ago,' he wrote to Ludwika on the 10th. 'There are only 300 tickets at 20 francs each. I shall have the cream of Parisian society. The King has commanded that ten tickets should be taken for him, the Queen ten, the Duchess of Orléans ten and the Duc de Montpensier ten, although the Court is in mourning† and none of them will be present.' 'My thoughts are occupied with my concert,' he told his mother the next day. 'People have written to my publisher from Brest and from Nantes to reserve places. I am astonished at such *empressement* [eagerness], and today I must play, if only for conscience' sake, for I believe I am playing worse now than ever before… There will be no posters and no free tickets… Pleyel always jokes about my stupidity, and will decorate the steps with flowers to make me more willing to play. I shall be as if at home, and my eyes will meet scarcely any but familiar faces.' With Franchomme and the violinist Jean-Delphin Alard (Sarasate's future teacher at the Conservatoire), he played a Mozart piano trio (the late E major, K. 542) and the last three movements of the Cello Sonata. Among solo pieces, offered in a gentle, restrained fashion, were the Berceuse, the Barcarolle, a nocturne and some waltzes, mazurkas, preludes and studies. He was so frail and unwell that Hallé, one of the few to attend the concert, relates in his *Autobiography* how he played the Barcarolle 'from the point when it demands the utmost energy [following the middle section], in the opposite style *pianissimo*, but with such wonderful nuances that one remained in doubt if this new rendering were not preferable to the accustomed one'.

Low with influenza, and with social and political tensions running high in Europe, Chopin found himself drawn increasingly to an invitation from one of his Scottish pupils, Jane Wilhelmina Stirling (older by six years, and dedicatee of

* Translated Bernard Jacobson.

† The mourning period for Adélaïde, including the cancellation of balls and receptions in the city, lasted officially until 25 January – but Chopin's remarks suggest that it was observed for longer, certainly at Court.

the Op. 55 Nocturnes), to visit her and her widowed sister, Mrs. Katherine Erskine, in Scotland. The inadvisability of such a trip notwithstanding, his mind was made up a few days later. To the strains of the *Marseillaise* beneath a 'sombre and threatening sky', an insurrection broke out in Paris on the 'disagreeable' morning of Tuesday the 22nd – the 'working-class militants' of the metropolis claiming their 'right of popular resistance to oppression as part of the revolutionary tradition of Paris since 1789' *.

Fuelled by the suppression of the *campagne des banquets* (private political meetings)… the outlawing of gatherings and demonstrations… a *petite bourgeousie* grown angry during the economic crisis and depression of 1846–47, when the harvest failed… and the union of Republicans and liberal Orleanists, the so-called *Révolution de Février* voiced terminal dissatisfaction with Louis-Philippe and the July Monarchy. Come the mid-forties his government had become increasingly corrupt and autocratic, those in positions of authority reaping countless benefits at the expense of others less fortunate. By February 1848, 'cold and rainy', reform and the removal of the royal house was on the lips of everyone, even members of the National Guard. 'Word was given that the whole system must fall,' and that the prime minister, François Pierre Guillaume Guizot, had to go. Bayonets drawn, horses at the ready, soldiers guarding the Ministry of Foreign Affairs stood by their orders…

Below: Jane Wilhelmina Stirling (1804-59), the faithful guardian of Chopin's legacy. She owned his last piano, purchased from Pleyel's hire fleet (No. 14810). In 1982 the many scores he altered, elaborated or annotated for her were published in facsimile by the Bibliothèque nationale.

* William Fortescue, *France and 1848: The End of Monarchy* (London 2005).

[37-43 Boulevard des Capucines, 2nd/9th *arrondissement*, 23 February, late afternoon] A gun was heard, and the 14th Regiment of Line levelled their muskets and fired. The scene which followed was awful. Thousands of men, women, children, shrieking, bawling, raving, were seen flying in all directions, while sixty-two men, women, and lads, belonging to every class of society, lay weltering in their blood upon the pavement. Next minute an awful roar, the first breath of popular indignation was heard, and then flew the students, artisans, the shopkeepers, all, to carry the news to the most distant parts of the city, and to rouse the population to arms against a government whose satellites murdered the people in this atrocious manner. A squadron of *cuirassiers* [armoured cavalry] now charged, sword in hand, over dead and wounded… fathers snatching up their children, with pale faces and clenched teeth, hurried away to put their young ones in safety, and then to come out in arms against the monarchy. Women clung to

The Paris Revolution, Place de la Bastille, February 1848. 'I found in the capital a hundred thousand armed workmen formed into regiments, out of work, dying of hunger, but with their minds crammed with vain theories and visionary hopes. I saw society cut into two: those who possessed nothing, united in a common greed; those who possessed something, united in a common terror. There were no bonds, no sympathy between these two great sections; everywhere the idea of an inevitable and immediate struggle seemed at hand. Already the bourgeois and the people (for the old nicknames had been resumed) had come to blows, with varying fortunes, at Rouen, Limoges, Paris; not a day passed but the owners of property were attacked or menaced in either their capital or income: they were asked to employ labour without selling the produce; they were expected to remit the rents of their tenants when they themselves possessed no other means of living' - Alexis de Tocqueville

railings, trees, or to the wall, or fell fainting on the stones… The wounded, and those bodies which were claimed, were borne to houses in the neighbourhood [the National Guardsmen to town halls]… Seventeen corpses, however, were retained and placed upon a cart. Ghastly was the spectacle of torch and gaslight, of that heap of dead, a few minutes before alive, merry, anxious, full of hopes, and perhaps, lofty aspirations for their country. Round about were men, no less pale and ghastly, bearing pikes and torches, while others drew the awful cartload along *.

'This tragic event,' reported the same witness, 'sealed the fate of the Orleans dynasty.' Guizot, having earlier resigned at 2 o'clock (along with his cabinet), escaped to Belgium, arriving in London a week or so later. On the 26th, two days after Louis-Philippe's

* Percy Bolingbroke St. John, *The French Revolution of 1848* (London 1848).

abdication, a provisional government, the Second Republic, was formed, with Lamartine appointed minister of foreign affairs and Sand in the role of muse, 'spin doctor' and general banner waver. In December the formerly imprisoned, long-exiled Louis Napoléon Bonaparte was elected president, France's first. The democracy, however, proved short-lived (as Balzac predicted it would be). On 2 December 1852, favoured or fixed by a 97% vote, *le Prince-Président* became Emperor Napoléon III, tinselled ruler of the Second Empire. One of the first acts of his elevation was to ship political prisoners to Devil's Island and New Caledonia.

Half a mile from the Boulevard des Capucines, Chopin was languishing in bed, an attack of neuralgia on the way. 'Paris,' he wrote to Solange (3 March), 'is quiet, with the quiet of fear. Everyone has rallied to the cause of order. Everyone has joined the National Guard. The shops are open – no customers [more than half were to close in the coming months]. Foreigners, passports in hand, are waiting for the damage to the railways to be repaired. Clubs are beginning to be formed. But I should never stop if I tried to tell you what is going on here… That Louis Blanc should be at the Luxembourg as president of the Labour Commission (employment being the real burning question of the moment) – that is quite natural.'

Delacroix's chronicles of the day haven't survived: his 1848 diary was lost in a cab hailed at Gare de Lyon. But in his *Memoirs* – in the wake of *les journées de Juin*: a bloody stand-off between workers and authority, armed insurgents and a punishing military machine, that led to thousands of deaths and, for many, banishment to Algeria – Berlioz left a graphic account of the city's state by high summer:

[16 July] Paris is burying her dead. The pavements used for the barricades have been replaced—to be torn up again, perhaps, tomorrow. The moment I arrive I go straight to the Faubourg Saint-Antoine. A hateful scene of destruction; even the Spirit of Liberty on top of the Bastille column has a bullet through her body. Trees mutilated or overthrown, houses crumbling, squares, streets, quays—everything still seems to vibrate under the shock of bloody disorder. Who thinks of art at such a time of frenzy and carnage? Theatres shut, artists ruined, teachers unemployed, pupils fled; pianists performing sonatas at street corners, historical painters sweeping gutters, architects mixing mortar on public building sites. The Assembly has just voted a sum

Manet's *The Folkestone Boat,*
Boulogne, 1869.

large enough to enable the theatres to reopen and to afford
a little relief to the most hard-hit artists. Inadequate relief,
above all to the musicians! A first violin at the Opéra was
lucky if he earned nine hundred francs a year; he lived by
giving lessons. It is hardly to be supposed that he could
have saved on a very brilliant scale. Now their pupils have
gone, what is going to happen to such people? They won't
be deported, though for many of them their only chance
of making a living would be in America, India or Sydney.
Deportation costs the government too much. To qualify,
one must have deserved it, and our artists all made the
mistake of attacking the barricades and fighting against
the insurgents.

Surrounded by this ghastly confusion of justice and
injustice, good and evil, truth and falsehood, hearing a
language spoken whose words are perverted from their
normal meaning, what is to prevent one from going
completely mad?*

* Translated David Cairns.

146

With his social world pulverised and thoughts darkened by another Polish uprising (in Poznań), Chopin packed his bags and after a fairly rough Channel crossing arrived in Folkestone on the evening of 20 April at six o'clock. Rested, he reached London the next day, Good Friday, to be met at London Bridge station by Jane Stirling and her sister, who had arranged for some expensive rooms to be placed at his disposal at 10 Bentinck Street, Marylebone. The following week, through the agency of Adam Czartoryski and the Polish Government in Exile, he moved into a lavishly furnished suite of rooms at 48 Dover Street just off Piccadilly*, a stroll across Green Park from Buckingham Palace, his drawing room large enough to accommodate three grand pianos – his Pleyel (No.13819) sent by special delivery from Paris, a hand-picked Broadwood (No. 17093), and an Érard on loan from the maker. He soon acquired five students, attractive wealthy women more anxious to call themselves his pupil than further artistic gifts of their own. His fee was a guinea a lesson – which he needed, for by June his rooms alone were costing him 'ten guineas a week (for once I was settled and had sent out my cards, the rent was raised)', a figure close to £800 by today's standards. Yet if the cost of living worried him, he had a supportive admirer in Jane, who saw to his every whim (even 'my drinking-chocolate') – but whose stifling generosity was eventually to deprive him of space and atmosphere.

Would 'you meet her in private life, you would not notice her… She must be seen when her countenance is lighted up with the inspiration of her art, and then, possibly, you might pronounce her beautiful. Her eyes flash with the light of her genius. Her lips part with the inspiration of her song… All is life and animation' (Charles G. Rosenberg, New York 1850). The grey-eyed obsession of Hans Christian Andersen and Felix Mendelssohn. Within days Chopin was at the Haymarket Theatre, two-and-a-half guinea ticket in hand, to see Jenny Lind, younger by ten years, in Bellini's *La Sonnambula* (4 May) – 'a typical Swede, not in an ordinary light but in some Polar dawn'. He warmed to her. 'Yesterday [12 May] I was at dinner with J[enny] Lind, who afterwards sang me Swedish airs till midnight. They are as distinctive in character as our things. We have something Slavonic, they something Scandinavian, which are totally different; and yet we are nearer to each other than the Italian to the Spaniard' † [pp. 148-49]. The Easter weekend, Parisian in ambience, was spent in Richmond with 'some people belonging to the former King's [Louis-Philippe's] entourage'.

* Home in 1906 to Fabergé's first London gallery, and then in 1917 to the British School of Osteopathy, No. 48 was destroyed during the Second World War.

† In *Chopin and the Swedish Nightingale* (Brussels 2003), Cecilia & Jens Jorgensen generalise/propose an intimacy – physical, platonic or spiritual – missed or un-noted by Chopin's chroniclers. Certainly, it seems, the two spent time in each other's company, chaperoned or otherwise, her modest (long vanished) London cottage in rural Old Brompton (latter day South Kensington), with its plane trees and magnolias, offering a possibly much needed private refuge. 'Whatever is NOT boring is NOT English,' Chopin wrote on 17 July. 'Chopin and Jenny Lind developed a close relationship,' hypothesise the Jorgensens. 'Over several months, they spent considerable time together in London and Scotland, and they talked marriage.' Enigmatic references, coded symbols, and puzzling innuendos apparently inform their letters to others (nothing survives between them). Coincident with a week seeing Chopin in Edinburgh, Lind obtained blank marriage allegation papers from London, stamped 28 September 1848. Days later, in Dublin, she broke off her engagement to her long-standing Swedish beau. On 30 October, Chopin wrote to Gryzymała: 'the unmarried one [interpreted widely, given the context, to mean Jane Stirling, but by the Jorgensens to indicate Lind – both qualify for the label] is far too much like me. How can one kiss oneself?… Friendship is friendship, I have made that clear, but it gives no claim to anything else. Supposing that I could fall in love with someone who loved me in return, and as I would wish to be loved, even then I would not marry, for we should have nothing to eat and nowhere to live. But a rich woman looks for a rich husband and if she does choose a poor man he

Fragile constitution aside, Chopin's letters cheerily reveal his surroundings, and his rapid introduction to a British aristocracy living 'on names and grandeur' ('every evening I am out'). To Adolf Gutmann, serving in the National Guard, he writes that 'all the Parisian pianists come here [but the public] want classical things. Thalberg has been engaged for twelve concerts in the same theatre where Lind appears. Hallé is going to play Mendelssohn…' (6 May). Mendelssohn, who'd died prematurely from a 'nervous stroke' the previous November in Leipzig, was all the rage. Benefitting from his standing with Queen Victoria, he was virtually the only foreign composer to then command such popularity. His music figured everywhere, not only in the Promenade Concerts of Jullien but also in the programmes of the prestigious Philharmonic Society, founded in 1813. Offering the most important orchestral platform in the land, the Society was keen to engage Chopin. He wasn't drawn, writing to Grzymała (Saturday 13 May):

The day after tomorrow the Duchess of Sutherland is to present me to the Queen, who will visit her *in gratiam* for a christening. If the Queen and Prince Albert, who know about me, should be pleased it will be good, for I shall begin from the top. I have been offered the Philharmonic, but don't want to play there because it would be with the orchestra. I have been [to the Hanover Square Rooms] to observe. Prudent played his [B flat] Concerto [on 1 May], and it was a fiasco. Here one must play Beethoven, Mozart or Mendelssohn, and although the directors and others tell me that my concertos have already been played [the must not be a feeble creature, but young and vigorous. A man on his own can struggle along, but when there are two, poverty is the greatest misfortune. I may give up the ghost in an institution, but I won't leave a wife to starve.' The following week, early November, the two conceivably met in London. And definitely so in May and June 1849, when, with her advisers, she visited Paris. 'A drama of Shakespearean proportions' – she, 'the one from the North', 'immensely' in love with someone 'I was very near to marrying' (11 July 1849)… only to have her nerves 'shattered'. To the end of her life she sang Chopin, she played his music – but 'never confided on paper what I did not think should be known to the world' (15 June 1880).

* Rated the most valuable private property in 1840s London, renamed Lancaster House in 1912, this palatial neo-classical mansion on The Mall accommodated the London Museum from 1914 through to the Second World War.

F minor in April 1843, the Romance and Rondo of the E minor in March 1844], and with success, I prefer not to try, for it may come to nothing. The orchestra [conducted by Michael Costa, a busy, autocratic Neapolitan] is like their roast beef or their turtle soup: excellent, strong, but nothing more. All that I have written is needless an excuse; there is one impossible thing: they never rehearse, for everyone's time is costly nowadays. There is only one rehearsal, and that is in public.

Knowing his limitations and what he wanted, Chopin was being pragmatic. Others, though, including Davison of *The Times*, 'a creature of the late Mendelssohn' and a vocal Chopin disparager, took offence at the perceived 'insult'.

On May 15th – along with Julius Benedict and the lionised bass-baritone-tenor gods Lablache, Tamburini and Mario

– Chopin was presented to Victoria and the Prince Consort at Stafford House, St. James's *, home of Harriet, Duchess of Sutherland, one of whose daughters, Lady Constance (not yet fourteen), was taking lessons from him. In a long letter to his family (around 4,500 words, written on pale blue sheets decorated with engraved views of Edinburgh, 10-19 August) he described the occasion:

The Duchess of Sutherland had the Queen to dinner, and in the evening there were only eighty persons belonging to the most exclusive London society. Besides the Prince

Queen Victoria (1819-1901): oil portrait by Franz Xaver Winterhalter, 1842.

of Prussia (who was to leave London shortly) and the royal family, there were simply such people as old Wellington and so on (though it is hard to find a parallel). The Duchess presented me to the Queen, who was amiable and talked with me twice. Prince Albert, an enthusiastic amateur musician and composer, came up to the pianoforte. Everyone told me that both these things are rare… I should like to describe to you the Duchess of Sutherland's palace but I can't. All the royal palaces and castles are old: splendid, but neither so tasteful nor so elegant as Stafford House (as the Duke of Sutherland's palace is called)… for instance, the staircases are famous for their magnificence. They are neither in the entrance nor in the vestibule, but in the middle of the rooms, as if in some huge hall with the most magnificent paintings, statues, galleries, hangings and carpets: of the loveliest design, with the loveliest perspective. On these stairs one could see the Queen, under a brilliant light, surrounded by all sorts of bediamonded and beribboned people with the Garter, and all descending with the utmost elegance, carrying on conversations, lingering on various levels, where at every point there is some fresh thing to admire. It is true one regrets that some Paul Veronese could not see such a spectacle, so that he could have painted one more masterpiece.

How he played isn't chronicled, but Charlotte von Rothschild (from the Naples-Frankfurt branch of the family) heard him on the 12th at Lady Antrobus's house, 146 Piccadilly, before his rendezvous later that evening with Jenny Lind:

Chopin came into the room with great effort; he looked ghostlike, could hardly speak, and with every word his eyes filled with tears, his frail body twitched convulsively; he is extraordinarily thin, and yet it seemed to me as if there was not a bone in his body… I cannot tell how much I wondered at the unsurpassable delicacy of his playing, which no other fingers could match, and his glittering interpretation; one could truly have imagined one was hearing shimmering pearls falling gently onto the keys. Such soft, gentle, delicate, tender, sweet playing has surely never been perfected before.

Confounding popular expectation though not the political

barometer – the Whig government in Westminster being 'hostile to the Polish cause' – Chopin was not invited to the Palace. Nor, whatever the rumours (reaching as far afield as Paris), did the Queen ever become his pupil. 'Some pretty music... some pianists playing' was the extent of her diary entry for the 15th.

Chopin's income came from teaching and appearances at the homes of the nobility for whom, Henry Broadwood decided (some thought rashly), he would play for a fee of 20 guineas (around £1600 in modern equivalence), and where he could meet men of letters like as Dickens and Carlyle. The first of these paid engagements was on May 24 at Lady Gainsborough's, 9 Cavendish Square*. Two semi-public concerts were additionally arranged for 23 June and 7 July with seats at a guinea each, earning him a further three hundred pounds or so. The first of these events, the guests including Jenny Lind, was a *matinée* at 99 Eaton Place, the Belgravia residence of Mrs. Adelaide Sartoris, younger daughter of the actor Charles Kemble; but it was less successful than the second, at Lord Falmouth's mansion, 2 St. James's Square (bombed in the Blitz, 14 October 1940). A similar programme was offered on both occasions, including the Second Scherzo, Berceuse, and sundry delicacies. At Falmouth's – 'a fervent lover of music, rich and celibate...you might give him a few pence if you passed him in the street... his house is full of servants who dress better than he does' – Pauline Viardot joined him in French settings she'd made of some of the mazurkas (later taken up by Jenny Lind, who sang them at Windsor and the Palace during the 1855/56 season). The London *Daily News* for 10 July commented:

> [Chopin] accomplishes enormous difficulties, but so quietly, so smoothly and with such constant delicacy and refinement that the listener is not sensible of their real magnitude. It is the exquisite delicacy, with the liquid mellowness of his tone, and the pearly roundness of his passages of rapid articulation, which are the peculiar features of his execution, while his music is characterised by freedom of thought, varied expression and a kind of romantic melancholy which seems the natural mood of the artist's mind.

His listeners resorted to verse. An army captain, one Anthony Coningham Sterling, a future veteran of the Crimea campaign, 7 July:

* See Rose Cholmondeley, *Chopin's Visit to Britain*, bicentenary talk for the Chopin Society UK, Royal Festival Hall, 1 March 2010, online transcript *http://www.chopin-society.org.uk*.

Like a chant of the fairies
The harmony varies
With long drawn whisperings
Out of life's hidden springs,
Till the pale wizard waking
With every nerve shaking
Pours a last peel of thunder
That leaves us in wonder—
So his magical fingers
With exquisite skill
Make a music that lingers
In memory still—

By the end of July London society had done its entertaining. With Europe in strife, making travel abroad unwise, the aristocracy, following royal example, headed up to Scotland for the summer break, coinciding with the start of the shooting season. Chopin, out of pocket to one of his students for nine unpaid lessons, slipped into another 'black day' phase. 'My nerves are in tumult, he tells Grzymała in a letter resumed several times (8-17 July). 'I am no longer capable of sadness or joy – I have used up my feelings completely – I only vegetate and wait for it to end more quickly'. He thinks of Solange and Sand. Mademoiselle de Rozières, too – now 'a good sort'. Pondering his 'kind Scottish ladies,' he frets that 'they bore me so much that I don't know which way to turn. They absolutely insist on my going to stay with their family in Scotland: that might be nice, but today I have no desire for anything'.

His three months in the capital hadn't all been gilt-edged. He'd discovered that people, out for a bargain or a favour whatever their station, were 'not so open-handed and money is tight everywhere'. 'These English are so different from the French, to whom I have grown attached as to my own; they think only in terms of pounds; they like art because it is a luxury; kind-hearted, but so eccentric that I understand how one can himself grow stiff here, or turn into a machine.' He'd witnessed strong anti-Polish feeling. 'No one bothers over the Irish and Carlist questions… people here are more concerned with the state of things in Paris, Italy and Poland, about which [the latter] *The Times* recounts such fantastic things that even the English are amazed at its ill will' (2 June). As for music, it was as cheap as small-talk, double-speak and the non-committed answer. The 'attention [of the upper class] is frittered away so much on a thousand different trifles, they

Above: Jenny Lind (1820–87): steel engraving by Jacques-Marcel-Auguste Hüssener. The goddess of an age, loved by many. 'I have brightness in my soul, which strains toward Heaven. I am like a bird!'

are so hemmed in by tiresome conventions, that it's all the same to them whether the music is good or bad, for they are compelled to listen to it from morning till night. There is music at every flower-show, music at every dinner, every sale is accompanied by music. The *Savoyardów* [street entertainers], *Czechów* [Bohemians] and my [pianist] colleagues are as numerous as dogs, all mixed up together'.

Courting critics and promoters before loyalty and integrity – never Chopin's style – was a political dynamic for many. 'In Viardot's programmes at present (yesterday at the Palace, for instance [29 June]), there is no longer the item "Mazurkas of Chopin" but merely "Mazurkas arranged by Mme. Viardot". It appears that it looks better. It is all the same to me; but there is a pettiness behind it. She wants to have success [competing with Jenny Lind, not all her London reviews had been favourable] and is afraid of a certain newspaper which perhaps does not like me. It once wrote that she had sung music "by a *certain* Mr. Chopin" whom no one knows, and that she ought to sing something else.'

Across the rainy weeks* his physical and mental condition had worsened. On his own admission his moods were 'horrible'. He sketches cemeteries, crosses and tombs in his diary. He spits blood. Reduced to little more than six stones, he is an invalid who has to be carried down steps, carried off coaches, carried into hotels. 'I cannot breathe if I have to climb stairs'. The spectacle must have been distressing. Then there were his linguistic limitations, making it impossible to express himself or grasp the finer nuances of what was being said to him. 'Although everyone in high society speaks French, especially the ladies, the general conversation is mostly in English, and I then regret that I don't know the language; but I have neither the time nor the desire for it. I understand simple things; I can't starve or come to grief; but that is not enough' (10-19 August).

* 1848 was a wet year in Britain, with high rainfall in June and August. Before Chopin's arrival the Thames had flooded around Reading, reported in *The Times*, 4 March, ahead of a news item on 'The Fighting in Paris' and 'the pool of blood that flowed from the victims of the firing at the Hôtel des Capucines' (see pp.143-44).

12 Alba

'Within [Chopin] there is so much love, poetry, reason, greatness, tenderness, that one completely forgets about people, about the world, about him'

Zofia Rosengardt

An invitation from Lord Torphichen, Jane's elderly brother-in-law, provided the necessary excuse to leave London at the beginning of August. On Saturday the 5th, accompanied by his new French-speaking Irish man-servant, Daniel ('a better person than many gentlefolk, and handsomer than many Englishmen'), and a Broadwood-appointed Scottish manager, John Muir Wood, he boarded the 9 o'clock morning 'express' from Euston to Edinburgh Lothian Road, via Birmingham and Carlisle, occupying two first-class seats. The 407-mile journey took a damp, draughty, smoky, rattling twelve hours. After a two-day rest at Douglas's Hotel, 34-35 St. Andrew Square – 'one of the most fashionable in the city' according to *Cassell's Old and New Edinburgh*, and where Walter Scott had stayed in 1832 – he left 'exquisite' Edinburgh for Calder House, the 16th century Mid Calder estate of Torphichen, a carriage being especially provided – 'harnessed in the English style, with the driver mounted on horse'.

In the letter to his family of 10-19 August Chopin pictured the place as he first saw it:

> It is an old manor [in former times – John Knox's day – 'a great palace'] surrounded by an enormous park with ancient trees; you can see only lawns, trees, mountains and sky. The walls are eight feet thick; there are galleries on all sides, dark corridors with endless numbers of ancestral portraits, of various colours, in various costumes – some in kilts, some in armour, and ladies in farthingales – everything to feed the imagination. There is even some kind of *chaperon rouge* [apparition] which appears, but which I have not seen. Yesterday I looked at all the portraits, but I have not seen which one it is that

Calder House.

wanders about the castle. The room which I inhabit has the most beautiful view imaginable—towards Stirling, beyond Glasgow, and to the north fine scenery... there is nothing I can think of that does not at once appear: even the Parisian newspapers are brought to me every day. It is quiet, peaceful and comfortable... [Torphichen] has asked me to come for the whole summer next year; they would let me stay for the rest of my life...

Communing with Ludwika in Polish, he was spiritually back in Warsaw and 'happy'. The weather was 'fine'. 'The park has a wonderful light on it—it is morning'. But though he resisted to 'think about the winter till it is imperative to do so,' the need to generate money to meet his expenses and cover his rent and taxes in Square d'Orléans was a worry:

> ... at the very beginning of October they want me to play in Edinburgh. If it will bring in something, and I am strong enough, I shall gladly do it, for I don't know how to turn round this winter. I have my lodging in Paris as usual, but don't know how to make ends meet. Many persons want me to stay in London for the winter,

in spite of the climate. I want something else, but don't myself know what. I will see in October, according to my health and my purse, for an extra one hundred guineas in my pocket would do no harm… If I were younger, perhaps I would go in for a mechanical life, give concerts all over the place and succeed in a not unpleasant career (anything for money!); but now it is hard to start turning oneself into a machine.

On 18 August, he sits at his table writing to Fontana, then briefly in London on his way back to New York (where he had settled in 1845):

We are two old cembalos on which time and circumstances have played out their wretched trills. Yes, *two old cembali*, even if you protest at being included in such company—that means no disparagement to beauty or respectability. The *table d'harmonie* is perfect, only the strings have snapped and some of the pegs are missing. The sole trouble is this: we are the creation of a celebrated maker, a Stradivarius of his kind, who is no longer there to mend us. In clumsy hands we cannot give forth new sounds and we stifle within ourselves all those things which no one will ever draw from us, all for lack of a repairer. I can hardly get my breath: I am just about ready to give up the ghost... I am vegetating, patiently waiting for the winter, dreaming now of home, now of Rome; now of joy, now of grief.

On the 25th Chopin took the 10.30 morning train to Salford to give a Gentlemen's Hall 'Dress Concert' in Peter Street, Manchester, billed for the 28th 'at seven o'clock precisely'. '200 and something English miles, 8 hours, railway journey'. Fee: 60 guineas – £5,000 in today's terms. Audience: 1200. Piano: his favoured London Broadwood (No. 17047*). In the 1840s Manchester (Roman Mancunium) was a bustling city, a spearhead of the industrial revolution, and a centre of political reform. But it lacked the elan of royal Edinburgh, and was sootier, darker and smellier than London. Spared its grimmer, grimier side, he stayed at Crumpsall House close to rural Middleton, the recently acquired seat of the 'kind' Salis [Salomon ben Elias] Schwabe. Manufacturer, calico-printer (he owned the vast Rhodes Works) and humanitarian, Schwabe,

* The Cobbe Collection Trust, Hatchlands, Surrey, on permanent loan from the Royal Academy of Music. Hatchlands additionally hold Chopin's so-called 'English' Pleyel (No. 13819), *c* 1846 – which before returning to Paris in July 1848 he sold to one Lady Trotter for £80 (around £7,000 today) – and Jane Stirling's December 1842 Érard (No. [15]713), which he used in Scotland during his stay at Keir House.

contemporaries reported, together with his wife Julia, was a man devoted to 'the comfort and intellectual furtherance' of his work force, his ideas on education, enlightenment, morality and welfare 'a century before his time'. A Westphalian Jew who'd come to Britain in 1817, converting to the Unitarian Church, 'epitome of all that was refined, benevolent, tolerant, and high-minded,' Schwabe was noted for his patronage of the arts, his friends including Jenny Lind (who stayed within days of Chopin)*, Charles Hallé and Wagner, the Carlyles, Mrs. Gaskell, George Eliot and Florence Nightingale. A frequent house guest was the Austrian-born composer Sigismund von Neukomm from Paris, one of Louis-Philippe's circle. 'Haydn's best pupil,' Chopin reported enthusiastically, '[who] used to be court conductor to the Emperor of Brazil, you must have heard his name.' A key figure in the Europeanisation of Manchester, Schwabe was against the extreme left, decrying the socialist movement: his middle son, George Salis-Schwabe, five at the time of Chopin's stay and a future Lieutenant Governor of the Chelsea Royal Hospital, was elected Liberal MP for Middleton in the 1885 General Election. Making way for urban development, Crumpsall House was demolished in 1934. Dismantled brick by brick (more than a million-and-a-half of them), the landmark 1846 chimney of the Rhodes Works, 358 feet high – noted by Chopin as 'the biggest chimney in Manchester [Europe, too, for a while], costing £5,000 [£380,000]' – stood until 1982†.

Tantamount to a whisper in a large gallery, Chopin's Manchester solos, including the Berceuse and Fourth Ballade, were interleaved between arias and ensembles by Verdi, Pacini, Rossini Bellini and Donizetti, with lightweight overtures by Weber, Beethoven and Rossini completing the programme. 'A fragment of great beauty' thought the *Manchester Courier*. The correspondent for the *Musical World*, though, was less immediately enthralled (9 September):

> Mons. Chopin's pianoforte playing… neither surprised me, nor pleased me entirely. He certainly played with great finish—too much so, perhaps, and might have deserved the name of *finesse* rather—and his delicacy and expression are unmistakable; but I missed the astonishing power of Leopold de Meyer, the of Thalberg, the dash of Herz, or the grace of Sterndale Bennett. Notwithstanding, Mons. Chopin is assuredly a great pianist, and no one can hear him without receiving some amount of delectation.

* In 1852 Lind married Otto Goldschmidt, 'a very amiable young man' and pianist from Hamburg, who was a relative of Mrs. Schwabe.

† The author is grateful to Colette A. Wagstaffe for her research into the Schwabe family *http://www. middletonia.co.uk* (March 2010).

Returning to Edinburgh Chopin spent a night at his *poste restante*, 10 Warriston Crescent – the residence of Adam Łyszczyński, a homoeopathic doctor 'who has married well, lives in tranquillity and has become quite English'. From here he went to Johnstone Castle, twelve miles west of central Glasgow, the 'fine and luxurious' home of another of Jane Stirling's sisters, Anne, and her husband Ludovic Houston, the local laird.

Contending with Jane, unwilling to requite any feelings she may have had for him, was by now becoming stressful. She met the bills, strove hard to see that her delicate, famous luminary was comfortable and nursed, and aimed to re-create the kind of atmosphere she supposed to have once existed at Nohant. But Chopin was weary of her fussing and the parochial company her friends and family kept:

I am cross and depressed, and people bore me with their excessive attentions. I can't breathe; I can't work; I feel alone, alone, alone, although I am surrounded... Here it's nothing but cousins of great families and great names that no one on the Continent has ever heard of. Conversation is always entirely genealogical, like the Gospels; who begat whom, and he begat, and he begat, and he begat, and so on for two pages till you come to Jesus... There are a whole lot of ladies, seventy- to eighty-year-old lords, but no young folk: they are all out shooting. One can't get out of doors because it has been raining and blowing for several days [to Grzymała, 4-9 September].

A visit to Edinburgh by Princess Marcelina Czartoryska – one of the Radziwiłłs and a Paris pupil of Chopin's (having previously studied in Vienna with Czerny) – accompanied by her husband, provided needed relief. 'I came to life a little under their Polish spirit: it gave me strength to play in Glasgow where some dozens of the nobility assembled to hear me.' On the 25th he went to a performance of *La Sonnambula*, with Lind in her celebrated rôle as Amina.

Under the conscientious management of Muir Wood, 'numerously attended by the beauty and fashion, indeed the very elite of our West End', the Glasgow *matinée* took place on Wednesday 27 September, a 'fine' afternoon, at the Merchants [Hutcheson's] Hall, 158 Ingram Street, 'to commence at half past two o'clock' (in the event thirty minutes later to accommodate arriving carriages). Playing a Broadwood 'of most exquisite tone', Chopin – 'a little fragile looking man, in pale grey suit, including frock-coat of identical tint and texture... occasionally consulting his [miniature] watch' – offered his usual programme of shorter, less taxing pieces, including the Berceuse, Nocturnes Opp. 27 and 55, and Second Ballade (no doubt truncated as he was accustomed to do, with the bravura *presto con fuoco* sections omitted). 'It was a drawing room entertainment,' the poet James Hedderwick remembered over forty years later, 'more *piano* than *forte*, though not with occasional episodes of both strength and grandeur. He took the audience, as it were, into his confidence, and whispered to them of zephyrs and moonlight rather than of cataracts and thunder. Of the whirl of liquid notes he wove garlands of pearls.'

Following a formal dinner at Johnstone Castle, Chopin headed for Keir House near Dunblane, the imposing seat of

Edinburgh, from St. Anthony's Chapel, Holyrood Park. 'The ancient and famous metropolis of the North sits overlooking a windy estuary from the slope and summit of three hills. No situation could be more commanding for the head city of a kingdom; none better chosen for noble prospects. From her tall precipice and terraced gardens she looks far and wide on the sea and broad champaigns. To the east you may catch at sunset the spark of the May lighthouse, where the Firth expands into the German Ocean; and away to the west, over all the carse of Stirling, you can see the first snows upon Ben Ledi. But Edinburgh pays cruelly for her high seat in one of the vilest climates under heaven. She is liable to be beaten upon by all the winds that blow, to be drenched with rain, to be buried in cold sea fogs out of the east, and powdered with the snow as it comes flying southward from the Highland hills. The weather is raw and boisterous in winter, shifty and ungenial in summer, and a downright meteorological purgatory in the spring. The delicate die early ...' - Robert Louis Stevenson, *Edinburgh: Picturesque Notes* (London 1878/79).

one of Jane's lowland relations, William Stirling - a dilettante pianist whom Chopin knew from London, and a wealthy, widely travelled young bachelor and authority on Spanish art. A letter to Grzymała, dated 1 October – the Sabbath day, strictly observed – is headed 'Perth Shire. Sunday. No post, no railway, no carriage (even for a walk); not a boat, not even a dog to whistle to':

> … the future grows always worse. I am weaker, I
> can't compose anything, less from lack of desire than
> from physical hindrances… the whole morning, till 2
> o'clock, I am fit for nothing now; and then when I dress,
> everything strains me, and I gasp that way till dinner
> time. Afterwards one has to sit two hours at table with the
> men, *look* at them talking and *listen* to them drinking.
> I am bored to death (I am thinking of one thing and
> they of another, in spite of all their courtesy and French
> remarks at table). Then I go to the drawing room, where
> it takes all my efforts to be a little animated—because
> then they usually want to hear me… then my good Daniel
> carries me up to my bedroom (as you know that is usually
> upstairs here) undresses me, gets me to bed, leaves the
> light; and I am free to breathe and dream till it is time to
> begin all over again. And when I get a little bit used to it,

then it is time to go somewhere else for my Scottish ladies give me no peace; either they come to fetch me, or take me the round of their families (*nota bene*, they make their folk invite them constantly). They are stifling me out of *courtesy*, and out of the same *courtesy* I don't refuse them.

'My Scottish ladies'. Katherine, for ever bereaved. Jane, for ever spinstered. Sisters in black from a brood of thirteen, Calvanists of the realm, chaste mistresses of blood-line and etiquette, living a life where the unbridled, the physical liberty of the moment, was to be borne but not indulged. To Grzymała, shortly before returning to Paris, Chopin pictures Mrs. Erskine as 'a very religious Protestant, a good soul, [who] would perhaps like to make a Protestant of me; she brings me the Bible, talks about the soul, quotes the Psalms; she is religious, poor thing, but she is greatly concerned about my soul. She is always telling me that the other world is better than this one; and I know all that by heart, and answer with quotations from Holy Scripture' (17-18 November). 'A hoarse-voiced, restless, invalid Scotch lady, of some rank,' says Thomas Carlyle of Jane, 'mostly wandering about on the Continent, entertaining lions, and Piano Chopin, &c., &c., but always swooping down upon London and us now and then'. 'So pale and grave—like the *widow* of Chopin — so friendly, and unconscious, to all appearance, of my dislike to her' (Jane Carlyle, 4 August 1850).

Privy to lightweight news, 'Derozierka' – de Rozières – gets

Hamilton Palace, 1916, ancestral seat of the Dukes of Hamilton.

a cameo to be shared chattily (2 October), Chopin communicating upper class rhythms with a painter's eye for scene and swift perspective:

> … country-house life in high society is really very interesting. They have nothing like it on the Continent… there are about thirty other people [here at Keir], some very beautiful, some very witty, some very eccentric, some very deaf, and even [one] who is blind. There are fine dresses, diamonds, pimply noses, lovely heads of hair, marvellous figures, the beauty of the devil himself and the devil minus the beauty! This last category is the commonest to be found wherever one goes. They are all going to Edinburgh today for the Caledonian Rout. All this week there will be race-meetings, entertainments, balls, etc. The local fashionable set, the Hunt Committee, arrange these *fêtes* every year. All the local aristocracy puts in an appearance.

'Monsieur Chopin Has The Honour/to announce that he will give a/SOIREE MUSICALE/in Edinburgh, on the evening of/Wednesday, the 4th October.' He arrived at Łyszczyński's the previous day, basked in the 'fine, even warm' weather, and took time to see Jenny Lind off at the station, *en route* for Glasgow, then Dublin. His last full-length concert in public, the two-hour recital, tickets at half-a-guinea, took place at 8.30 in the Hopetoun Rooms (today 70-72 Queen Street): *à la* Liszt, but exceptionally for the period, he bore the responsibility for the programme himself without the aid of a singer or supporting artists. The 'gem of this performance', for the informed critic of the *Edinburgh Advertiser* (6 October), was the Berceuse, 'the most popular' a selection of mazurkas and waltzes. 'His manner of playing… was quite masterly in every respect [contrasting the] Donner und Blitzen school of pianists [which] has thrown most European young ladies into fits of ecstatic admiration, and into a career of insanely ambitious imitation' (*The Scotsman*, 7 October). 'Like the dying swan, he must have given of his best' (Rose Cholmondeley).

Wracked with 'cough and suffocation,' all energy expended, Chopin returned to Calder House. He thinks of Gutmann in Germany, writing on the 16th:

When I lately read of the disturbances in Heidelberg,
I began a lot of letters to you, and ended by burning
them all… Ever since you last wrote to me, I have been
in Scotland, Walter Scott's beautiful country, among
all the memories and reminders of Mary Stuart, of the
Charleses, etc. I visit one lord after another. Everywhere I
meet, together with the heartiest goodwill and boundless
hospitality, superb pianofortes, magnificent paintings,
famous collections of books; there are also hunting, dogs,
dinners without end, cellars, for which I have less use.
It is difficult to conceive of the refinement of luxury and
comfort that one meets in English castles… Everything
here is doubly brilliant, except the sun, which is the same
now as always; the winter is already approaching, and
what will happen to me I don't yet know. I am writing
from Lord Torphichen's… I walk about [the corridors]
with my doubts. The cholera approaches; London is full
of fogs and spleen, and in Paris there's no president, no
president.

A few days followed at Hamilton Palace, South Lanarkshire
(demolished in the 1920s), as guest of the Duke and Duchess of
Hamilton. The old Whig – former ambassador to the Russian
court, Napoléon admirer, Masonic Grand Master, Trustee of
the British Museum, a gold-ringed dandy in his youth, 'the
proudest man in England' – was noted for his deportment and
guardsman bearing. 'He was always dressed in a military laced
undress coat, tights and Hessian boots' (Alexander, 1st Baron
Lamington). 'A duke in boots and spurs, buckskin breeches with
a kind of dressing gown over everything' (Chopin). Egyptian
mummies obsessed him (on his death in 1852 he was, at his
request, mummified and placed in a Ptolemaic sarcophagus
he'd acquired in Paris in 1836). He collected paintings, books
and manuscripts, in 1811 taking the unlikely (no doubt to
some unpatriotic) step of commissioning David's *The Emperor
Napoleon in His Study at the Tuileries*. His estates included the
Isle of Arran. He enjoyed good company and laughter. Among
fellow house guests of Chopin were the Prince and Princess of
Parma, Ferdinando and Ludwika, then exiled near London, 'a
very gay young couple'. From Hamilton Palace Chopin wrote to
Grzymała on the 21st – penning an astute summary of all that
he'd encountered, experienced and been frustrated by during his
months in Britain:

Art, here, means painting, sculpture, and architecture. Music is not art and is not called art; and if you say an artist, an Englishman understands that as meaning a painter, architect or sculptor. Music is a *profession*, not an art, and no one speaks or writes of any musician as an artist, for in their language and customs it is something else than art: it is a *profession*. Ask any Englishman and he will tell you so... No doubt it is the fault of the musicians, but try, to correct such things! These queer folk play for the sake of beauty, but to teach them decent things is a joke. Lady —, one of the first *great ladies* here in whose castle I spent a few days, is regarded as a great musician. One day, after my piano, and after various songs by other Scottish ladies, they brought a kind of accordion, and she began with the utmost gravity to play on it the most atrocious tunes. What would you have? Every creature here seems to me to have a screw loose. Another lady, showing me her album, said to me, 'La Reine l'a feuilleté et je me trouvais alors juste à côté d'elle' [I stood by the Queen while she looked at it]. A third that she is 'la 13ème cousine de Marie Stuart' [thirteenth cousin of Mary Stuart]. Another, *standing* up for the sake of originality, and accompanying herself on the piano, sang a French-English romance with an English accent: 'j'aie aiiemaiie' (j'ai aimé), pronounced J'ay ay-may!!! [I have loved]. The Princess of Parma told me that one lady whistled for her with a guitar accompaniment. Those who know my compositions ask me, 'Jouez-moi donc votre *second* Soupir [Nocturne Op. 37 No. 2]—j'aime beaucoup vos cloches' [play me your second Sigh—I love your bells]. And every observation ends with 'leik water', meaning that it flows like water. I have not yet played to any English woman without her saying to me 'Leik water'!!! They all look at their hands, and play the wrong notes with much feeling. Eccentric folk, God help them.

Weakened by a further chill on the sixty-mile journey back to Edinburgh, he arrived at Warriston Crescent and the welcoming arms of Dr. Łyszczyński on the 30th. To Grzymała, 'My dearest Life':

Have you forgotten me, that you read into my letters — in which I wrote that I am progressively weaker, duller,

without any hope, without a home — you read that I
am to get married?... I [have written] a sort of list of
instructions [will] for the disposal of my bits of things if
I should expire here... I have not seen [my Scotswomen]
for two or three weeks, but they are coming today. They
want me to stay, and go on dragging round the Scottish
palaces, here there and everywhere... They are kind, but
so boring that the Lord preserve them... wherever I go,
they come after me if they can. Perhaps that has given
someone the notion that I am getting married; but there
really has to be some kind of physical attraction... I am
not thinking at all of a wife, but of those at home, my
mother and sisters... What has become of my art? And
where have I squandered my heart?...This world seems to
slip from me, I forget things, I have no strength. If I rise
a little, I fall again, lower than ever... I am nearer to a
coffin than a bridal bed... I am resigned...

The next day Chopin returned by train to London, and
Henry Broadwood's house at 33 Great Pulteney Street. By
3 November he was settled into 4 St. James's Place, not the
brightest, most open of streets ('we light the candles at two
o'clock'). On Thursday the 16th, at the invitation of Lord Dudley
Coutts Stuart, a pro-Polish independence activist married to
Princess Christine Bonaparte living a few doors opposite at No.
34, he left his sick-bed to appear at the 'Annual Grand Dress
and Fancy Ball and Concert in aid of the Funds of the Literary
Association and Friends of Poland' hosted in the Guildhall. A
Broadwood 'repetition grand' was placed at his disposal, the
same 1847 rosewood-veneered 80-note instrument he'd played
at Eaton Place and Lord Falmouth's in the summer (No. 17047).
The event, needing police protection, divided opinion, *The
Times* on the day calling it 'a bitter mockery upon the sufferings
of the English poor':

In France sympathy with Poland has been a pretext
for sedition – in England an excuse for morbid
sentimentality. In the one country it has meant bayonets,
in the other balls... Job Smith and Abel Brown are out of
work and are hungry – they, their wives, and they're little
ones... Their names terminate neither in *owsky* nor *itzky*
– were it so [they] might stand a better chance... There
are no flags nor banners, no lamentations for the past,

nor anticipations for the future. Job and Abel must go to the relieving officer, if they can stagger to the workhouse door, and there obtain – just as much as they can get… we think numerous instances might be found amongst the dancers and spectators at the Polish Ball tonight of good-natured but careless people, who never troubled themselves with the thought of whether or no they had done their duty by their countrymen, before casting their superfluity to aliens and strangers.

'Chopin played like an angel,' Marcelina Czartoryska wrote to her uncle in Paris the next day, 'much too well for the inhabitants of the City, whose artistic education is a little problematic.' For one observer 'a well intentioned mistake,' his patriotic contribution went largely unrecognised if not unheard. 'The concert took place in the Council Chamber… The qualities which give [Chopin] his special charm are too delicate and intellectual to challenge the favour of a crowd bent chiefly on physical enjoyment' (*Sun*, 17 November). He never played again on stage. 'I have ended my public career.'

To Grzymała, 17-18 November:

I have been ill the last eighteen days, ever since I reached London. I have not left the house at all, I have had such a cold and such headaches, short breath, and all my bad symptoms… I don't care about anything… I have never cursed anyone, but now my life is so unbearable that it seems to me it would give me relief if I could curse Lucrezia [George Sand]—but no doubt she also suffers, suffers all the more because she will doubtless grow old in anger. I am endlessly sorry for Sol[ange]… My kind Scottish ladies are boring me again.… If I were well, with two lessons a day, I should have enough to live comfortably here; but I'm weak: in three months, or four at the outside, I shall eat up what I have *.

Recognising there was nothing more they could do, conscious that pollution and smog, and the dankness of the Thames at Westminster, was exacerbating his condition ('I can neither breathe nor sleep'), his doctors, including the Queen's Scottish Physician-in-Ordinary, Sir James Clark (a specialist in pulmonary consumption), urged him to return home.

* On returning from Scotland Chopin opened an account at Coutts in the Strand, depositing £250 – around £22,000 in modern equivalency.

Instructions to prepare his rooms at Square d'Orléans were sent to de Rozières and Grzymała, emphasising the need for everything to be aired and dusted ('especially those [curtains] around my bed'), and requesting a plentiful supply of logs and fir-cones ('so that I can get warmed right through as soon as I arrive'). 'Tell Pleyel to send me any kind of piano… [get] a bunch of violets to scent my drawing-room – let me find a little poetry.' Driven 'mad' by the Stirlings, linguistically crippled for so long, he allows himself just a glimmer of boyish excitement: 'I can't wait for the time when I shall be able to breathe more easily, understand what people are saying, and see a few friendly faces'.

13 Marche funèbre

'A man of exquisite heart and mind'

Delacroix

* Consumption – tuberculosis – is the traditionally accepted reading of Chopin's and Emilia's condition. But both cystic fibrosis and alpha-1 antitrypsin deficiency, inherited disorders associated with reduced life expectancy, have been suggested in recent medical research. According to Grzymała, Chopin was 'convinced that medical science had never understood his disease'; the autopsy report, since lost, 'found that the cause of death had been different from what was thought [the death certificate gave tuberculosis of the lungs and larynx], but nevertheless he could not have lived'. Permission to carry out DNA testing on Chopin's preserved heart was refused by the Polish government in 2008. See J. A. Kuzemko, 'Chopin's Illnesses', *Journal of the Royal Society of Medicine*, December 1994; W. N. Arnold, 'Chopin's Heart', *Hektoen International*, January 2011; Steven J. Lagerberg, *Chopin's Heart* (n.p., 2011). Temporal lobe epilepsy has been proposed to explain his wider neurological symptoms from Mallorca onwards – the seizures, periodic lapses of recognition, 'cohorts of phantoms', 'cursed creatures' and 'walking dead', the moments of suddenly pale countenance and 'wild eyes and hair on end'. See Manuel Vázquez Caruncho & Franciso Brañas Fernández, 'The hallucinations of Frédéric Chopin', *Medical Humanities*, 24 January 2011.

On the morning of Thursday 23 November 1848, seen off by the Czartoryskis, Chopin, his face swollen with neuralgia, departed 'this hellish London,' travelling by train to Folkestone via Reigate and Tonbridge, accompanied by Daniel his man-servant and a Polish friend, Leonard Niedźwiedzki – with an extra seat booked for him to put up his feet. Lunch with wine, probably at the well-patronised Pavilion Hotel – opened in 1843 'for passengers using the New Commercial Steam Packet Company's service to Boulogne' – was followed by an hour-and-three-quarter sea crossing. Chopin, who'd begun the day with a nervous seizure, ended it delivering his repast to the waves. The following morning the ragged party left Boulogne, arriving in Paris around noon. Chopin, watching the countryside unfold, turned to Leonard: 'Do you see that cow in the meadow? *c'a à plus d'intelligence que les Anglais*' ('it has more intelligence than the English').

He faced a year ridden and stigmatised with consumption, the disease that had claimed his sister Emilia and taken away so many friends dear to him *. Musically he was barren. 1847-48 had been empty years, a kerchief of reminiscences, sketches and unfinished ideas scattered sparodically. A 'Jewish' nocturne, the Ogiński-redolent Waltz in A minor (another for Mrs. Erskine, 12 October 1848, in B major, still unpublished), a mazurka. The lingering germ perhaps of something (a scherzo, a sonata?) for violin and piano. Now and again he'd scribble his reduction of *Wiosna*, his 'stock' autograph, into a music album – once for the late Mendelssohn's friend Sophie Horsley (London, 29 June 1848); once for Fanny Erskine, a relative of Katherine's related to the Earls of Mar (Crumpsall House, 1 September 1848).

The first half of 1849 was spent in intimate company – Delacroix, the poet and essayist Cyprian Norwid, the 'enchantress' Delfina Potocka. Sand enquires after his health from Pauline Viardot. 'He has some bearable days, when he is able to travel by carriage, and others when he is spitting blood and has attacks of coughing that choke him. He no longer goes out in the evening. However, he is still able to give a few lessons, and on good days can even be cheerful... He speaks of You with the utmost respect... he *never does otherwise*' (15 February). In mid-May Solange breathlessly tells him, 'mon petit Chopin,' that she's had another daughter, Jeanne *(sic)*, 'as huge as the other was tiny'. Delacroix's journal noted the days – intellectually more reviving than many for some months:

> *Monday 29 January* Alarms since early morning, on account of the mutiny of the *garde mobile*. Went to see Chopin in the evening... stayed with him until ten o'clock. The dear fellow! We talked of Mme Sand, of her strange life and extraordinary mixture of virtues and vices... Chopin says that she will never be able to write [her *Mémoires*]. She has forgotten the past; she has great outbursts of feeling and then forgets very quickly.

> *Friday 2 February* In the evening I talked music with Chopin, Grzymała and Alkan. He thinks that Beethoven was obsessed by the idea of Bach.

> *Friday 9 February* He gets very indignant to see mediocrities appropriating the ideas of the masters and either ruining them, or else sickening people with the way they use them.

> *Saturday 7 April* Went with Chopin for his drive at about half-past three... The Champs-Élysées, l'Arc de l'Étoile, the bottle of quinquina wine, being stopped at the city gates etc.... We talked of music and it seemed to cheer him... He made me understand the meaning of harmony and counterpoint... that to be well versed in the fugue is to understand the elements of all reason and development in music... science, as regarded and demonstrated by a man like Chopin, is art itself...

> *Saturday 14 April* To see Chopin in the evening; I found him in a state of collapse, scarcely breathing... He said that boredom was the worst evil he had to suffer...

> *Sunday 22 April* To Chopin after dinner. He is another man it does one's heart good to be with, and one's mind as

well, needless to say… He had dragged himself out to see the first performance of Meyerbeer's *Le Prophète* [Salle le Peletier, 16 April, Viardot in the rôle of Fidès]. His horror at that rhapsody!*

In June, forced to accept that no matter where he went, in his state of health, Paris was a frightful place – 'thirty-six kinds of weather, plenty of mud, draughts in the room. Nothing goes: for the moment, everything is disgusting' (to Solange, 13 April) – Chopin moved for a few weeks to an apartment in Chaillot in the 16th *arrondissement*, Grande rue 74, then a rural suburban village 'a long way [from] town' (but *en route* by 'omnibus' from the Square), in the hope that the air and calm might do him good ('the *spring sunshine* will be my best doctor'), and that he would be spared the cholera outbreak which had claimed Kalkbrenner and Angelica Catalani within 48 hours of each other. 'I sit in the [first floor] drawing-room and admire my view over all Paris: the towers, the Tuileries, the Chamber of Deputies, St. Germ[ain] l'Aux[errois], St. Étienne du Mont, Notre Dame, the Panthéon, St. Sulpice, Val de Grâce, Les Invalides; from five windows, and nothing but gardens between' (to Ludwika, 25 June). 'Those who are very attached' came to visit – Pleyel, Gutmann, Lind, Potocka, Franchomme, the Rothschilds, the Czartoryskis, Cyprian Norwid, Zaleski. The small-talking 'Scots ladies' too – 'they will suffocate me'. 'I have not yet begun to play, and I cannot compose… I do not got out, except now and then [after dinner at five] to the Bois de Boulogne' (18 June). Whenever he left his rooms he had to be carried. His plight was upsetting. Potocka, Aix-la-chapelle, 16 July: 'It afflicts one to feel that You are so alone in Your illness and sadness… think seriously about Nice for the winter… The whole of this life amounts simply to one enormous discord'. From Nohant, three days later, fearful in the political climate of 'persecution or arrest' should she return to Paris, George Sand reminded her 'long and painful family story' to Amélie Grille de Beuzelin, 'without need to either justify or accuse myself': '… others have come between us… [he shows] in his attitude and looks an anger, even a hatred… I still hope he may live… but I have an inner conviction that he does not want [to see me]. His feelings died long ago, and if my memory torments him, it is because he feels pangs of conscience'.

Chopin had scarcely any pupils (most by now having passed on to his Russian assistant Vera Rubio or been recommended to nearby Alkan) and wasn't taking on new ones. No music had

*Translated Lucy Norton.

170

been published since the Cello Sonata in late 1847. Doctors' fees were draining him of resources. In May the Rothschilds helped with 1,000 francs. The following month his mother sent 1,200 from Warsaw. Chaillot was quietly funded by a third-party source. Then – in a 'drama' involving a 'stupid' concierge, Mrs. Erskine, and a young clairvoyant, Alexis Didier 'the "magnetic" somnambulist' – an anonymous sum of 25,000 francs in bank-notes (around £975: £85,000 in modern currency) turned up at Square d'Orléans, having *apparently* been left in a packet, but not delivered, on 8 March. 'I could not understand such munificent gifts from anyone, unless perhaps the Queen of England… You may take notice that I did not accept the *donation*; and that is enough about the matter' (to Grzymała, 28 July). The provenance of this philanthropic gesture, of which he was in the end persuaded to keep a portion (15,000 is noted in his diary), remains a mystery.*

In his June letter to Ludwika, Chopin urged her to come and see him – 'I am weak and no doctor can help me like You'. She arrived in Paris on 9 August, with her daughter and husband, Józef. He, however, true to the rancorous, unpleasant family man he was, returned to Warsaw soon after. His dislike and envy of Chopin, not to mention his mental cruelty towards Ludwika, was well known. Despite its evidently urgent nature, he'd withheld Chopin's letter for several weeks. He'd even refused to pay the travel costs to Paris, insisting that Chopin's aged mother settle the bill. She did, helped by Izabela and her husband, but at the expense of having to stay behind. Early in 1853, shortly before Józef's death, Ludwika began a letter to him – a frank insight into marital torment, sisterly anguish and Chopin's fading days. It stops thirty-two pages later, unfinished:

> You have lost faith in me, yet I never lied to you and you still say you are my best friend. Permit me, my dear, to make a most conscientious confession to you of all my actions, but do believe me, as you once used to, and then you may judge me with your heart and your mind. At the same time I am asking you, if you have still a true friendship and attachment towards me, may this confession remain between us two…
>
> When we arrived in Paris Fryderyk seemed to have gained a new lease of life, but all the time I saw how many things there used to annoy you, things which it was impossible to change—and I saw how often you were

* The Jorgenses, *op. cit.*, questioning Niecks's assertion, prevalent throughout the 20th century, that the money emanated from Jane Stirling, then living on £300 annually, favour the wealthier Jenny Lind to have been the source – 'it could have been nobody else'. Reference to the incident has for several years been suppressed from the biographical timeline of the Fryderyk Chopin Institute.

unforbearing to his little fancies and habits. Granted that it was out of your concern for me, but do admit how many times you were angry with me for sitting by his bed late at night, but many times you reproached him for preventing me from having enough sleep. I know it was dictated by your concern for me, but it was very painful to him, and a great tribulation for me, for I went there to look after him, to nurse him, to console him, to endure any hardship as long as it would bring him even the smallest relief in his sufferings—and he, poor thing, liked to talk late at night, to tell me all his troubles, and to pour into my loving and understanding heart anything that concerned him most…

If only you did not become so offended, if only would put yourself in my position—if only you would consider yourself a member of our family and be in harmony with us—if only you had thought of Fryderyk as a brother and mourned him together with us… you could have come here [for the funeral], helped me and acted to the advantage of us all; but you took offence, no longer remembered who it was who offended you and only thought how to take revenge on me. Judge for yourself if your action was just and noble…

… on many occasions when I talked to Fryderyk and he worried [about money], I asked him to put his mind at ease… I told him what my heart was dictating to me but with the knowledge that I would do everything in my power to help him…

… everybody [in Paris] knew that he [Chopin] had no debts. Since all people adored him and knew about his affection for us and ours for him, they thought it would be best for us to keep all the objects of which the transport would not cost too much, as souvenirs, and to dispose of the rest by selling them to Fryderyk's friends. Then I wrote to you and suggested that we keep the piano in the family and in that way have priority over others. To this you replied with one of the most hurtful letters which I ever had in my life: you ordered me to sell absolutely everything (for which you had to send me later a paper giving me authority to sell) and you added: 'sell everything, do not keep anything, anything at all,' and 'not one rag [of Chopin's] will I let into my house'. Oh, I wept tears of blood over this letter! Can you imagine the pain I felt in my heart, a pain which

I had to hide before strangers, because they were glad that I had a letter from you, being sure that your letter must have brought some comfort and relief to my heart. But all I could expect from all your subsequent letters was rubbing salt into my wounds, in spite of that affection which once existed between us. I could not understand you, indeed could you yourself understand your own motives for such tyrannical conduct?

You forbade me to take Chopin's nurse as a travelling companion and told me that you will not accept her into our house. It did not occur to you how difficult it was for me to travel alone with my child, in January [1850], prostrate with grief and hardly alive…

… you became more and more petty. Because [unkind] people told you that I can do with you what I want, you thought that these people had opened your eyes, so you decided to change it. While previously you were the undisputed master of the house now you became an absolute despot. You told our household that nobody else but you had the right to give orders here, that only your will was sacred. It was sufficient for me to be fond of any of the [female] servants to make you dislike her. You told me yourself on many occasions: 'It is enough that you are praising her, she is sure to be useless,' and 'As she is your favourite, I must be hard on her.' How did you expect that my orders would be obeyed at home, if after I issued an order the servants would ask me: 'Did the Master order it?' I felt that all these things, painful although they were, did not have their origin in you, but in your offended *amour propre* [self love] and in jealousy fanned by wicked people. Out of a friend you became a tyrant, and I out of a friend became a slave who had no right to ask any questions or to have any say in domestic matters. I could not even talk to you about the children in a manner which becomes parents having confidence towards each other…

… to all my sufferings one more was added: I ceased to believe in the existence of friendship, and came to the conclusion that God wanted to punish me with this disenchantment…*

* First published by Krystyna Kobylańska, Warsaw1968. Translated Adam Harasowski, 'Death and Auction in Paris', *Music & Musicians*, Vol XVII/vi, February 1969.

† Jerzy Peterkiewicz, *Cyprian Norwid: Poems, Letters, Drawings* (London 2000).

Younger by eleven years, 'at first misunderstood then ignored' by his compatriots†, Norwid, a newcomer to France's Polish population of 6,000, kept the dying Chopin company in Chaillot,

Chopin's salon, Place Vendôme 12, by
Teofil Kwiatkowski, autumn 1849.

sharing a meal or a bottle of Bordeaux sent by Franchomme.
Once the pair paid a fleeting call on Zaleski and his young son
in nearby Passy on the Right Bank – formerly Balzac's domain.
His prose-cycle *Black Flowers* (1856) time-suspended the Chaillot
days: 'I entered the room next to the drawing-room, where
Chopin slept, most grateful that he wished to see me, and found
him dressed but half-reclining… his legs swollen… His sister sat
with him, strikingly similar to him in profile… He, in the shade of
a deep bed with curtains, resting on pillows and bound in a shawl,
looked very beautiful, as always, displaying in the most ordinary
motions of life something absolute, something monumentally
drawn… a naturally idealised perfection of gestures'.

On 30 August - effectively house-bound, a carafe of Pyrenees
mineral water to hand - matters took a turn for the worst. Seven
doctors from Warsaw and Paris reached a concensus: 'they did
what they could: however, the illness was already too advanced,
and the patient too weak, for him to be saved' (Grzymała).
Two days later, in a letter to Ludwika, Sand enquired after
him: 'Some people write that he is much worse than usual,

Chopin's necropolis, Père-Lachaise, 20th *arrondissement*, 11th division, Line 1, Y, 20.

Chopin on his deathbed.

others that he is only weak and fretful as I have always known him. I venture to ask you to send me word, for one can be misunderstood and abandoned by one's children without ceasing to love them… Your memories of me must have been spoilt in your heart, but I do not think I have deserved all that I have suffered.' Ludwika didn't reply.

On 9 September Chopin was moved to the grandest square in Paris, to 12 Place Vendôme in the 1st *arrondissement*, north of the Tuileries Gardens – a sunny south-facing five-room mezzanine apartment, with kitchen and servant's quarters on the ground floor, rented by Delfina. Friends visited – 'too many satins and crowns' (Norwid), 'his adorers in ermine or rags' (Grzymała), 'the *grande dames* of Paris considering it their duty to faint in his room' (Viardot). Gutmann played Mozart, Teofil Kwiatkowski sketched, the 'Scottish ladies' fussed attentively. He 'prepared to resume his work,' Grzymała reported. 'His brain was teeming with music but he had not the strength to sit as the piano or even to hold a pen. What a heart-breaking sight it then was to see such a great genius intact and yet made barren by

175

purely physical helplessness and prostration!'. Early in October he asked for his unpublished and unfinished manuscripts to be destroyed. 'There are many works to a greater or lesser degree unworthy of me; in the name of the affection that You feel for me please burn them all except for the beginning of the [piano] *Méthode* [bequeathed by Ludwika to Marcelina Czartoryska in 1850]… The remainder without exception is to be consumed by the flames, since I have too great a respect for the public and do not wish for works unworthy of the public to become disseminated on my responsibility and in my name' (Grzymała).

The year had passed. On the 13th he received the Last Sacraments from Aleksander Jełowicki, a one-time insurgent. According to Viardot 'he found the strength to say a heartfelt word to cheer his friends. He asked Gutmann, Franchomme and other musicians to practise only good music: "do this for me – I am certain that I shall hear you – it will give me pleasure"'. Two days later Countess Potocka, faithful and fragrant, journeyed from Nice. In tears, accompanying herself at the piano, she sang, among her songs possibly Franchomme's prayerful re-working of the G minor Nocturne from the Op. 15 set to Thomas Aquinas's 'O Salutaris Hostia'. On the 16th, Franchomme and Marcelina played a fragment of the Cello Sonata.

Shortly before 2 o'clock in the morning of Wednesday 17 October 1849, in his 39th year, suffering a seizure, his Adam's apple protrudent, 'he passed into another life, smiling until almost the last minute' (Grzymała). 'Matka, moja biedna matka' – 'Mother, my poor mother' – he is said to have murmured. Many or few were at his bedside (accounts vary) – but certainly, it seems, Ludwika and Solange (holding his hand), maybe also Gutmann. Saturday 20 October, Normandy – Delacroix: 'It was after lunch that I learned of the death of poor Chopin. Strangely enough, I had a presentiment of it before I got up this morning… What a loss he will be! What miserable rascals are left to clutter the earth, yet that fine soul is extinguished!'

The funeral service, costing Ludwika 5,000 francs borrowed from Jane Stirling and Mrs. Erskine, took place on 30 October at the Madeleine. Lefébure-Wély played the E minor and B minor *Préludes* on the church's new Cavaillé-Coll organ, and Castellan, Viardot, Dupont and Lablache, together with the Conservatoire Concert Society, performed Mozart's Requiem – having first ensured their fees. 'To show you what a world we live in… the singers have asked for 2,000 francs before they will pay to Chopin the homage which their own self-respect ought

Right: Chopin's death-mask by Auguste Clésinger.

to have impelled them to offer and not to sell to his memory'
(Grzymała). By way of *introit*, the Funeral March from the B
flat minor Sonata circled and echoed in an orchestration by
Napoléon Henri Reber. The long procession, led by Meyerbeer
and Prince Adam Czartoryski, the uncrowned monarch of
emigré Poland, with Prince Alexandre Czartoryski, Delacroix,
Franchomme and Gutmann as pall bearers, made its way along
the *grands boulevards* to the cemetery of Père-Lachaise, 'the
cemetery in the east'. In silence, without speeches, Chopin's
embalmed body was laid to rest near Cherubini and Bellini, not
far from Sébastien Érard. On returning to Warsaw Ludwika
smuggled past the Russian authorities, hidden within her skirt,
a hermetically-sealed crystal urn containing her brother's heart
preserved in alcohol, probably cognac, to be immured in a pillar
of the Church of the Holy Cross in 1882. In 1850 a monument,
designed by Clésinger and made possible through a fund set
up by Pleyel, was unveiled in Père-Lachaise. It represented a
weeping Muse and broken lyre. A year later Jane sprinkled some
Polish earth over the grave.

The obituaries were sonorous. In London *The Illustrated
London News* (27 October) reported that 'one of the greatest
celebrities of this musical epoch has just expired in Paris:
Chopin is no more… He has been styled the *Ariel* of the piano;
but he was also its *Prospero* – a mighty magician, inventing
imagery, flowing like an impetuous torrent, whilst his hands
were a tornado aggregating the subjects and investing them
with piquant and picturesque colouring, alternately pathetic and
gay, as his fancy dictated'. Cyprian Norwid's, written the day
after his friend's death, was the most intense (*Dziennik Polski*,
25 October). 'A Varsovian by birth, a Pole in his heart, a citizen
of the World… a man who could pick wild flowers without
disturbing the gentlest dewdrop, the softest pollen. Through
the art of the ideal he transformed them into the stars, the
meteors, the comets of a whole enlightened Europe. Through
him, in crystals of particular harmony, the tears of the Polish
people scattered across the fields gathered to become a beautiful
diamond in the diadem of humanity.'

Heroes are born, legends are made…

*'So intimate, this Chopin, that I think his soul
Should be resurrected only among friends –
Some two or three, who will not touch the bloom
That is rubbed and questioned in the concert room'*

T. S. Eliot

Select Bibliography

Abraham, G. *Chopin's Musical Style* (Oxford 1939)

Attwood, W. G. *The Parisian Worlds of Frédéric Chopin* (New Haven & London 1999)

Berlioz, H. trans. Cairns, D. *Memoirs* (London 1969)

Branson, D. *John Field and Chopin* (London 1972)

Delacroix, E. ed. Wellington H., trans. Norton, L. *The Journal of Eugène Delacroix* (London & New York 1951, 1995)

Goldberg, H. *Music in Chopin's Warsaw* (Oxford 2008)

Hallé, C. ed. Kennedy, M. *Autobiography* (London 1972)

Harasowski, A. *The Skein of Legends around Chopin* (Glasgow 1967)

Hedley, A. *Chopin* (London 1947 rev. Brown, M. J. E. 1974)

Hedley, A. *Selected Correspondence of Fryderyk Chopin* (London 1962)

Hipkins, E. J. *How Chopin Played* (London 1937)

Huneker, J. *Chopin: The Man and His Music* (New York 1900)

Iwaszkiewicz, J. *Chopin* (Kraków 1955)

Jonson, E. A. *A Handbook to Chopin's Works* (London 1905)

Kallberg, J. *Chopin at the Boundaries* (Cambridge, Mass. 1996)

Kobylańska, K. trans. Grece-Dąbrowska, C. & Filippi. M. *Chopin in his own Land* (Kraków 1955)

Kobylańska, K. *Chopin na obczyźnie* (Kraków 1965)

Lenz, W. trans Baker, M.R. *The Great Piano Virtuosos of Our Time* (New York 1899 [Berlin 1872])

Liszt, F. trans. Waters, E. N. *Frédéric Chopin* (New York 1963)

Marek, G. & Gordon-Smith, M. *Chopin: A Biography* (New York 1978)

Maurois, A. trans. Hopkins, G. *Lélia: The Life of George Sand* (New York 1953)

Methuen-Campbell, J. *Chopin Playing* (London 1981)

Niecks, F. *Frederick Chopin as Man and Musician* (London 1888)

Opieński, H. trans. Voynich, E.L. *Chopin's Letters* (London 1932)

Samson, J. *Chopin* (Oxford 1996)

Samson, J. *The Music of Chopin* (Oxford 1985)

Samson, J. (ed.) *The Cambridge Companion to Chopin* (Cambridge 1992)

Sand, G. *Histoire de ma vie* (Paris 1855)

Sand, G. trans. Graves, R. *Winter in Mallorca* (Valldemossa 1956)

Schumann, R. trans. Ritter, F. R. *Music and Musicians: Essays and Criticisms* (New York 1876)

Simeone, N. *Paris: A Musical Gazetteer* (New Haven & London 2000)

Sydow, B. E. *Correspondence de Frédéric Chopin* (Paris 1953)

Szulc, T. *Chopin in Paris* (New York 1998)

Walker, A. (ed.) *Chopin: Profiles of the Man and the Musician* (London 1966)

Willis, P. *Chopin in Britain: Chopin's visits to England and Scotland in 1837 and 1848* (doctoral thesis Durham University 2009)

Załuski, I. & P. *The Scottish Autumn of Frederick Chopin* (Edinburgh 1993)

Załuski, I. & P. *Chopin's Poland* (London & Chester Springs 1996)

Zamoyski, A. *Chopin* (London 1979)

Zamoyski, A. *Chopin: Prince of the Romantics* (London 2010)

Zebrowski, D. (ed.) *Studies in Chopin* (Warsaw 1973)

Catalogues

Brown, M. J. E. *Chopin: an Index of his Works in chronological order* (London 1960 rev. 1972)

Chomiński, M. C. & Turło T. D. *Katalog dzieł Fryderyka Chopina* (Kraków 1990)

Grabowski, C. & Rink, J. *Annotated Catalogue of Chopin's First Editions* (Cambridge 2010)

Kobylańska, K. *Frédéric Chopin Thematische-Bibliographisches Werkverzeichnis* (München 1979)

Online Sites

Chopin's First Editions Online [CFEO] *http://www.cfeo.org.uk*

Chopin: Kaleidoscope *http://kalejdoskop-chopin.pl*

Fryderyk Chopin Institute, Warsaw *http://www.chopin.nifc.pl*

Fryderyk Chopin Society, Warsaw *http://www.chopin.pl*

Online Chopin Variorum Edition [OCVE] *http://www.ocve.org.uk*

Index

CD Track Listing

1. Nocturne No. 2, in Eb major, Op. 9 No 2
2. Étude No. 5, in Gb major, Op. 10 No. 5 [Black Key]
3. Étude No. 12, in C minor, Op. 10 No. 12 [Revolutionary]
4. Piano Concerto No. 2, in F minor, Op. 21 – III Allegretto vivace
5. Ballade No. 1, in G minor, Op. 23
6. Nocturne No. 8, in D flat major, Op. 27 No. 2
7. Prélude No. 15, in D flat major, Op. 28 No. 15 [Raindrop]
8. Mazurka No.23, in Dmajor, Op. 33 No. 2
9. Polonaise No. 3, in A major, Op. 40 No. 1 [Military]
10. Prélude No. 25, in C# minor, Op. 45
11. Sonata No. 3, in B minor, Op. 58 – IV Presto non tanto
12. Waltz No. 6, in Db major, Op. 64 No. 1 [Minute]
13. Fantaisie Impromptu in C# minor, Op. 66
14. Waltz No. 11, in Gb major, Op. 70 No. 1
15. 17 Songs, Op. 74 – No. 1 Życzenie [A Maiden's Wish]
16. Nocturne No. 20, in C# minor, Op. Posth.

Piano: Idil Biret
Track 4: Slovak State Philharmonic Orchestra, Košice, Robert Stankovsky conductor
Track 6: Sándor Falvai
Track 10: Irina Zaritskaya
Track 15: Olga & Natalya Pasichnyk